Beginning iOS Game Center and GameKit

For iOS, tvOS, and MacOS

Second Edition

Kyle Richter
Beau G. Bolle

Apress®

Beginning iOS Game Center and GameKit: For iOS, tvOS, and MacOS

Kyle Richter
Eagle River, AK, USA

Beau G. Bolle
Syracuse, USA

ISBN-13 (pbk): 978-1-4842-7755-3
https://doi.org/10.1007/978-1-4842-7756-0

ISBN-13 (electronic): 978-1-4842-7756-0

Managing Director, Apress Media LLC: Welmoed Spahr
Acquisitions Editor: Aaron Black
Development Editor: James Markham
Coordinating Editor: Jessica Vakili

Cover designed by eStudioCalamar

Cover image designed by Freepik (www.freepik.com)

Distributed to the book trade worldwide by Springer Science+Business Media LLC, 1 New York Plaza, Suite 4600, New York, NY 10004. Phone 1-800-SPRINGER, fax (201) 348-4505, e-mail orders-ny@springer-sbm.com, or visit www.springeronline.com. Apress Media, LLC is a California LLC and the sole member (owner) is Springer Science + Business Media Finance Inc (SSBM Finance Inc). SSBM Finance Inc is a **Delaware** corporation.

For information on translations, please e-mail booktranslations@springernature.com; for reprint, paperback, or audio rights, please e-mail bookpermissions@springernature.com.

Apress titles may be purchased in bulk for academic, corporate, or promotional use. eBook versions and licenses are also available for most titles. For more information, reference our Print and eBook Bulk Sales web page at http://www.apress.com/bulk-sales.

Any source code or other supplementary material referenced by the author in this book is available to readers on GitHub via the book's product page, located at www.apress.com/978-1-4842-7755-3. For more detailed information, please visit http://www.apress.com/source-code.

Printed on acid-free paper

This book is lovingly dedicated to my wife Elizabeth, who can always be found by my side and who has provided endless patience and understanding of my life choices and decisions, such as committing to authoring additional books.

—Kyle Richter

Dedicated to my wife, Deborah, for always being there to help me keep going and putting up with many hours of rubber ducking.

—Beau G. Bolle

Table of Contents

About the Authors

Kyle Richter started writing code in the early 1990s on the Commodore 64 and soon after progressed to a Mac SE. Since then, he has been dedicated to working exclusively with Apple products. Kyle is currently the CEO of MartianCraft LLC, a custom mobile software development shop. Kyle has been running software development companies since 2004. His company was behind the release of the first iOS trivia game, as well as the first mobile game to support true nonlocal multiplayer. His companies have been named to the Inc. 5000 fastest-growing companies in the world on three separate occasions. Kyle has worked on notable projects for some of the largest brands in the world. He is also a frequent speaker on software development and entrepreneurship, speaking at more than 200 events across the globe. In his spare time, he enjoys traveling, backcountry hiking, scuba diving, and cooking. He can be found on Twitter at @kylerichter.

Beau G. Bolle has been tinkering with technology as long as he can remember and has over 20 years of professional software development experience. He's worked on a wide variety of clients from startups to Fortune 500 companies on an even wider variety of projects including audio tools; social media apps; ecommerce, bug tracking, source control, and CRM systems; and enterprise apps. As CTO of MartianCraft, he is dedicated to creating an environment that fosters creativity and enables people to do their best work. In his free time, Beau enjoys traveling, camping, and hiking. He's an avid tabletop gamer and has recently taken up leatherworking.

Acknowledgments

Writing this book would not have been possible without the support and help of many people. Looking at the acknowledgments for any technical book shows that while there may only be one author, there are dozens of people needed to ship a technical book such as this. First, I would like to thank Jordan Langille of One Toad Design for taking time out of his busy schedule to provide the graphics for the sample program contained within.

I would like to extend a special thanks to everyone at MartianCraft for doing their jobs so well and professionally that I was able to find the available time to work on this book. In addition, I would like to extend a special thanks to Beau G. Bolle for his help bringing this revised edition to print.

Last but not least, I would like to thank the community as a whole. Never before in my life have I met such a supportive, outstanding group of people. From Cocoaheads and NSCoders to conferences and forums, everyone has always been of the highest caliber. It is often said of the Apple development community that two competing developers can be friends and share code and secrets among each other. Whenever I got stuck on a seemingly unsurmountable problem, there has always been someone there to help me through it. Throughout all my years of development and my travels across the globe, I have never met another group of people as awesome as the Apple development community, without whom I may have never shipped my first app.

Foreword: The Legend of Kyle, Game Hero

By Brent Simmons for Kyle Richter's book on writing games

You picked up the right book. You're awesome! You're awesome and you want to write games. Cool. If I wanted to learn to write games, what I'd do is park myself at Kyle Richter's house and make him teach me. But then we'd get distracted, and some friends would be in town, and we'd end up going out and I'd learn nothing. Lucky us, lucky you and me both—we have this book. Whew.

Let me tell you a bit about the author. Folks in the developer community will tell you that "Kyle Richter" is of course a pseudonym. You may recognize the name from one of Tom Clancy's novels: "Kyle Richter" is a highly trained, highly experienced covert ops agent who retired from service before turning 30 and who then made millions by creating simulations—games—out of the tangles he encountered in various undeclared theaters around the world and in low-earth orbit.

It's obvious, if you think about it—the name "Kyle Richter" is a transparent fiction. "Kyle" sounds like "Guile," and "Richter" is obviously a reference to earthquakes. A perfect name for a perfect game hero: smart, cunning, and dangerous. However, in the interest of comprehensiveness, I should point out that a small minority of people claim that "Kyle Richter" is actually an elite group of Ninja Valley Girl programmers. This claim has been investigated, and not a single shred of evidence has been found. Nothing. Our top people have looked, I assure you.

"Which proves the point," some say. "If they weren't ninjas, there'd be some evidence. Ergo, they're ninjas." (I should also point out that this theory and this faulty logic come from designers, not programmers. As Kyle would say: "I know, right?")

Since I know Kyle personally, I can clear this up. Let's take the superficial qualities first: Kyle is built like Thor, but has a decided height advantage. His cherry-red hair is so radiant you can tell when he's coming around the corner. Children, squirrels, and vegetarians often mistake his face for the sun.

And then there's the laugh, that laugh, which is, well, pleasant enough, I guess.

Anyway, what's important is his mind, how he thinks, how he communicates. In a recent conversation with him, he recounted how he handles firing employees and contractors. "The second I realize things aren't working out, then it's over," he says. (Kyle drags a hand across the throat here. I recoil in horror until he assures me he's just letting them seek their bliss elsewhere.) "No point in dragging it out," he says.

What that tells me is that he has no patience for nonsense, that he's highly practical, and that he has Vulcan-like emotional control. All of which are superb characteristics in a teacher, especially for technical topics. In other words, you want to learn how to write games without having to wade through a bunch of fluff and nonsense. That's where this book comes in. (Fluff and nonsense are strictly relegated to this Foreword. The rest of the book is information-packed and well-written.)

Not that Kyle is trigger-happy to fire people. He isn't. Quite the opposite. This industry is very short on talent, and Kyle, like everybody else, works hard to find good iOS developers. There aren't enough of them—so please learn what's in this book and help us all out!

At the same time, Kyle's knowledge and the contents of this book go beyond the merely technical. Kyle knows the history of games and what makes some successful and others not. You have questions. ("Longevity. Morphology. Incept dates.") The book has answers.

- Does your game need a leaderboard? See Chapter 3.

- How awesome is it to add a multiplayer element to your game? Find out in Chapter 5.

But the book is a technical book, and it has the goods, and the code and the explanations—even for the newest APIs. Chapter 8, for instance, talks about turn-based gaming via GameCenter. Not a ton of people are expert at this yet, much less expert enough to write about it. Kyle is, though, and it's in the book.

If, in the end, it turns out that Kyle is "just this guy, you know?"—and a good sport who's fun to tease, and not actually Thor-like—it doesn't matter, because this book is a gold mine. And I'm proud of him.

In the eternal words of George Clinton: "Nothing is good unless you play with it." By which I mean: read, learn, and play. The book is technical, but the things you make will be for play, and making those things should be like playing. Have fun!

In the immortal, sunny words of Kyle Richter (or "Kyle Richter"): "I know, right?"

Introduction

iOS is by far the most popular development platform in the world. With changes to how apps are developed on Apple TV and MacOS, sharing code between platforms has never been easier. As all of these platforms continue to skyrocket in popularity, adding additional rich features to your software is more important than ever. Game Center and GameKit provide an easy path for adding advanced functionality to your software with only a fraction of the work in the past.

Prerequisites

This book assumes that you have the basic skills and understanding required to create an iOS, Mac, or Apple TV app. The book also assumes that you have the background necessary to work with Xcode 13 or newer. There will be no primer on how to define methods and variables, install and launch Xcode, or create and work with new projects or classes. There are many excellent books on those topics such as *Beginning iPhone Development with Swift* by Apress. When you feel comfortable that you are ready to begin working with some of the more advanced framework technologies such as Game Center and GameKit, we assume that you have the basics mastered to a degree that allows you to move through this book without consulting other texts for help.

How This Book Is Organized

As you begin working through this book, you will notice that it is broken down into stand-alone chapters. Every effort has been made so that each chapter can be read independently of the others. If you have no experience with Game Center or GameKit yet, it is highly recommended that you read the first two chapters before skipping around, as they will provide you with the basic information on how to get Game Center and GameKit up and running in your development environment.

Each chapter follows along with a simple sample iOS game that is introduced in Chapter 1. Following along with the book from start to finish will walk you through the process of creating a fully functional Game Center– and GameKit-leveraged iOS game. In addition, each chapter will build onto a Game Center Manager class that is designed to be reusable across all of your projects.

If you already have a background in Game Center and GameKit and are looking for help on a specific technology, each chapter is designed to walk you through its covered technology, as well as provide samples on how to apply the technology to your software.

Required Software, Materials, and Equipment

To develop iOS, MacOS, or Apple TV software—and more specifically Game Center– and GameKit-based software—you will first need an Intel-based or ARM Mac computer running MacOS 11 (Big Sur) or newer. While you can develop on older versions of MacOS, it will not support the most up-to-date release of Xcode. You will also need a copy of Xcode, which you can download for free from the Mac App Store or at `http://developer.apple.com`. This book has been targeted to work with iOS 15.

In addition to the software and hardware requirements, you will also need a developer account provided by Apple. This account lets you build and test software on devices, as well as ship your finished product to the App Store. The software developer account is available for $99 USD a year and you can purchase yours at `https://developer.apple.com/programs/`.

CHAPTER 1

Getting Started with GameKit and Game Center

Welcome to *Beginning iOS Game Center and GameKit*! This book is designed to walk you through the process of adding GameKit and Game Center functionality into your iOS, Mac, or Apple TV apps and games. It is centered around a sample game built for iOS that you will be introduced to later in this chapter. You will find that most of the instructions are universal between platforms; however, if there is specific behavior for a platform other than iOS, they will be called out in the text.

If you have an existing app or game that you want to add GameKit or Game Center functionality to, you may substitute that project instead; I will try to use the most generic approach possible throughout the forthcoming chapters to make the functionality easy to implement.

This book is written as a reference and resource to aid you in the process of adding social gaming functions into your iOS, Mac, or Apple TV app. While I recommend you follow along from beginning to end to gain the most knowledge of the covered technologies, it is not a requirement. Every chapter is designed to stand on its own. You can skip ahead to the chapters that cover the material that is relevant to your project and quickly implement them into your software.

© Kyle Richter and Beau G. Bolle 2022
K. Richter and B. G. Bolle, *Beginning iOS Game Center and GameKit*,
https://doi.org/10.1007/978-1-4842-7756-0_1

When Apple announced GameKit on March 17, 2009, it was presented as an answer to the often-frustrating game style networking on iOS devices, which, until this point, had been challenging to say the least. GameKit added support for Bluetooth and local area network (LAN) as well as voice chat services. Shortly after, Apple announced the Game Center addition to GameKit as part of iOS 4.0. With the new SDK, Apple brought a wealth of new features—the Game Center being the most important to the scope of this book. Game Center largely stood untouched without major updates until 2020 when Apple released a significant update to the Game Center and GameKit frameworks.

Developers in the community have a tendency to think of Game Center as a stand-alone set of Application Programming Interfaces (APIs). This is a fallacy. Game Center is an integral part of GameKit. The two complement one another and work hand in hand. You will see an abundance of evidence of this in the following pages. For the purpose of this book, we are going to address both of these technologies together as GameKit; however, we may still refer to Game Center–specific functionality by its proper name.

Note   Despite their names, GameKit and Game Center are not designed for just games. Apple has in the past cracked down on Game Center technology being used in nongames. Some developers have received the following type of rejection email from Apple:

"The intended use of Game Center is to complement game apps or game functionality within an app. However, we noticed that your app does not contain any game play or game features."

These rejections seem to apply mainly toward the use of leaderboards and achievements in nongaming apps. The argument can easily be made that adding a leaderboard or achievement system to your app adds a gameplay element. If you happen to receive this rejection, you still have the option of appealing it. There haven't been any instances of rejection for using GameKit networking in any app to my knowledge. However, when dealing with guidelines for App Store approval, you should always consult the latest Developer Guidelines made available by Apple.

GameKit: An Overview

GameKit can be broken up into three individual sections: networking, Game Center, and voice chat. Though all of these services work together to create a single seamless environment, it can be helpful to look at each individually. While there might be overlap between sections, such as networking and Game Center, each section of GameKit can be broken down into a primary category. While these sections are not differentiated in the API, you may find it is useful to keep them separate while learning GameKit development.

Networking

Networking in GameKit allows you to send and receive data between "peers." GameKit networking also provides a connection protocol to connect to local clients that are found on your Wi-Fi network or locally using Bluetooth.

GameKit supports creating an ad hoc Bluetooth or local wireless network between two iOS devices; Game Center matchmaking also supports networking over the Internet supporting up to 16 players at once. GameKit networking is covered in Chapters 6, 7, and 8. Game Center matchmaking is covered in Chapter 5.

Game Center

Game Center itself handles authentication, friends, leaderboards, achievements, and invitations. In a sense, Game Center is providing the server services that are related to social interaction. It can also be argued that Game Center contains its own networking system. While this is true, we will be grouping that topic in the preceding section on networking, which is covered extensively in Chapter 5. Game Center technologies, such as leaderboards and achievements, are covered in Chapters 3 and 4.

Note   Game Center, in various articles of print and reference documentation, sometimes refers to the collective set of Game Center APIs as well as to the Game Center app itself.

Voice Chat

"Game Voice," as Apple often refers to it, allows any app (not just games) to provide voice communication over a network connection, commonly known as VOIP. The APIs handle the entire listening and playback of audio feeds for the user and provide services to handle connections, communications, errors, and disconnections. This technology is discussed in Chapter 10.

Sample Game: UFOs

In my experience, most developers are "experience-type" learners. This means that they learn best by doing, not by watching or listening. When I first started to learn how to program, I would copy source code out of code magazines line by line into a Commodore 64. The experience of physically typing in each line of code is what I believe made the information stick.

Listening to a lecture or watching someone else write code prevented me from retaining a good deal of the information. I can't imagine I would have stayed with this career path if lectures and demonstrations were my only ways of learning. This book is designed in the spirit of other experience-type learners.

The first thing we cover, before moving into GameKit itself, is working with the supplied sample game. The game, which we call "UFOs," is designed not to be an award-winning, addictive game, but rather to be simple enough that it can be thought of as any generic project. I have made every effort to reduce the amount of code to less than 300 lines. Although the game itself is simple, I feel that it is vital that every reader understands the code as if they wrote it themselves. This will allow you, as the reader, to detach yourself from the project itself and focus on the GameKit-specific information. We will start by playing the game and then looking at the source code.

Note   The source code for all the chapters, as well as the sample project, is available at `www.apress.com`.

UFOs: Understanding the Game

The first thing you need to do is open the base project that you downloaded from apress.com. Figure 1-1 shows the file structure for the project. We'll quickly run the game to see what it's like.

Name	^	Date Modified
▼ 📁 UFO		Today at 11:05 AM
⬜ AppDelegate.swift		Today at 10:59 AM
▶ 📁 Assets.xcassets		Nov 10, 2020 at 10:14 AM
▶ 📁 Base.lproj		Today at 11:02 AM
⬜ GameViewController.swift		Today at 11:05 AM
⬜ HomeViewController.swift		Today at 11:02 AM
⬜ Info.plist		Today at 10:00 AM
⬜ SceneDelegate.swift		Today at 10:59 AM
⬜ UFO.entitlements		Oct 7, 2020 at 11:31 AM
📄 UFO.xcodeproj		Today at 11:00 AM

Figure 1-1. *The file structure for the UFO sample project, as seen by the Finder*

To play the game, select Run from Product Menu bar. The game will launch to a generic screen with one button labeled "Play." Go ahead and select the Play button. You will be taken to the game screen, as seen in Figure 1-2; this screen may vary slightly depending on your selected test device.

The objective of the game is both typical and simple; tilt the device up/down or left/right to move your ship around the screen. Once you are positioned over a cow, tap anywhere on the screen and hold until the cow has been abducted. You are awarded one point for every cow you abduct. Like all the best games, there is no ending or way to "win." Every time you abduct a cow, a new one will be spawned.

Figure 1-2. *A look at the gameplay view from the UFOs sample project*

Now that you understand how the gameplay works, you can take a look at the source code that makes everything happen.

UFOs: Examining the Source Code

In your group tree, you will see the four class files we will be working with: `AppDelegate.swift`, `SceneDelegate.swift`, GameViewController.swift, and `HomeViewController.swift`. The group tree is shown in Figure 1-3. You will also notice a Main.storyboard file which contains the user interface elements of the project.

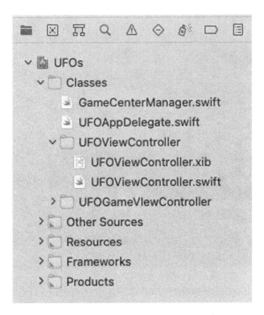

Figure 1-3. *A look at the group tree structure for the sample project from within Xcode*

First, take a look at the AppDelegate.swift and SceneDelegate.swift files. These files should look familiar to you from other swift development works. They are nothing more than a base UIApplicationDelegate and UIWindowSceneDelegate subclass. If you need to familiarize yourself with the code found here, take a look at Apple's sample code for new projects.

The next group of files is also relatively simple; take a look at UFOViewController.h and UFOViewController.m. These are the associated classes for the landing or home screen. All that we have here right now is a Play button, but we will be adding leaderboards, achievement, and multiplayer controls to this view as we progress through this book.

Finally, we will be working with UFOGameViewController.m. This is the main class that will be powering all gameplay and where the majority of the GameKit functionality will be added.

Setting Up the Accelerometer Delegate

The first thing our sample project needs to do is set itself up to detect accelerometer motion; the game will use this motion to move the players' spaceship. This code is found at the top of the GameViewController file. Take a look at the following code snippet, which is discussed in detail next:

```
private let motionManager = CMMotionManager()

override func viewDidLoad() {
    super.viewDidLoad()

    motionManager.accelerometerUpdateInterval = 0.05
    motionManager.startAccelerometerUpdates(to:
    OperationQueue.current!) { (accelerometerData, error) in
        self.motionOccurred(with: accelerometerData ??
        CMAccelerometerData())

        if error != nil {
            print(error.debugDescription)
        }
    }
}
```

The first thing we do is set motionManager to CMMotionManager(); this gives us a handy reference back to the main CMMotionManager. Next, viewDidLoad is overrode and code is added to set the accelerometer to test for new motion data every 1/20th of a second and then to call motionOccurred with the updated data, which we will discuss shortly. If there are any errors, they are then printed to the console.

Next, take a look at the additional variable definitions. Let's break this down into sections to understand exactly what is going on here:

```
private var movementSpeed = 15.0
private var accelerometerDamp = 0.3
private var accelerometerOAngle = 0.6
```

Here we set some class variables to hold onto some data that we will need when we begin to process the accelerometer input. We will be working with these variables again when we start to deal with ship movement. For now, you don't need to understand exactly what they are doing, just that they have been set.

Drawing the Player to the View

Next, we need to create our "player." At the top of the class file, you will find a definition for the playerImageView in which a share and initial starting position is first defined.

```
private let myPlayerImageView = UIImageView(frame: CGRect(x:
100, y: 70, width: 80, height: 34))
```

Shifting our focus back into the viewDidLoad function, you will find the following additional code snippet:

```
myPlayerImageView.animationDuration = 0.75
myPlayerImageView.animationImages = [
        UIImage(named: "Saucer1")!,
        UIImage(named: "Saucer2")!
    ]
myPlayerImageView.startAnimating()
view.addSubview(myPlayerImageView)
```

The next four lines of code are a little-known but very useful part of
UIImageView. We are setting an array of images that the UIImageView will
cycle through. In this example, we are setting two images to be rotated
through. We also specify how long we want the full animation to take
(3/4 of a second for our purposes) and the number of times we want the
animation to repeat. Once we have set up the animation details, we call
startAnimating() on the myPlayerImageView UIImageView. Then, all that
is left for us to do is add the UIImageView subview to the main view. Now
we have a player on the screen that is animating!

Setting Up Cows, Beams, and Scores

We have some objects to initialize and need to set up our score label.

```
private var cows: [UIImageView] = []
private let tractorBeamImageView = UIImageView()
private var score = 0
```

Once the variables are set up, we can once again turn our attention to
the viewDidLoad function and set the score variable we just defined to a
label that was created in the interface file.

```
scoreLabel.text = formatted(score: score)

for _ in 0..<7 { spawnCow() }
updateCowPaths()
```

The last thing we need to do in our viewDidLoad function is create
some cows for placement on the screen. I have created a helper function to
spawn these cows. Every time it is called, it will create a new cow and place
it on the screen. We will take a look at this a little later in this section. We
also call another helper function to update the walking path for the cows.
Again, we will look at this function in more detail later.

Adding Player Movements

That takes care of all our initialization and setup code. Now we can move into the more exciting parts of the game. First, we look at user input and actions and then the gameplay functionality.

```swift
func movePlayer(_ vertical: Double, _ horizontal: Double) {
    var vertical = vertical
    var horizontal = horizontal
    vertical += accelerometer0Angle

    if vertical > 0.50 {
        vertical = 0.50
    } else if vertical < -0.50 {
        vertical = -0.50
    }

    if horizontal > 0.50 {
        horizontal = 0.50
    } else if horizontal < -0.50 {
        horizontal = -0.50
    }

    var playerFrame = myPlayerImageView?.frame

    if (vertical < 0 && (playerFrame?.origin.y ?? 0.0) <
    120) || (vertical > 0 && (playerFrame?.origin.y ?? 0.0)
    > 20) {
        playerFrame?.origin.y -= CGFloat(vertical *
        movementSpeed)
    }
```

```
if (horizontal < 0 && (playerFrame?.origin.x ?? 0.0) <
440) || (horizontal > 0 && (playerFrame?.origin.x ??
0.0) > 0) {
    playerFrame?.origin.x -= CGFloat(horizontal *
    movementSpeed)
}

myPlayerImageView?.frame = playerFrame ?? CGRect.zero
}
```

The preceding function is much simpler than first glance would imply. The first chunk of code sets our maximum speed; we don't want the player to be flying around the screen too fast. The next section of code ensures that the user cannot move their UFO off the screen. Once we have checked both of these safety nets, we update the player's frame and move the UFO.

Watching for Touch Events

The next aspect of the game that we need to worry about is touch events. We will be using a touch to initiate and control the tractor beam. The first step is overriding the touchesBegan event.

```
override func touchesBegan(_ touches: Set<UITouch>, with event:
UIEvent?) {
    currentAbductee = nil
    tractorBeamOn = true

    if gameIsMultiplayer {
        gcManager?.sendStringToAllPeers("$beginTractorBe
        am", reliable: true)
    }
```

```
tractorBeamImageView?.frame = CGRect(x:
(myPlayerImageView?.frame.origin.x ?? 0.0) + 25, y:
(myPlayerImageView?.frame.origin.y ?? 0.0) + 10, width:
28, height: 318)
tractorBeamImageView?.animationDuration = 0.5
tractorBeamImageView?.animationRepeatCount = 99999
let imageArray = [UIImage(named: "Tractor1.png"),
UIImage(named: "Tractor2.png")]

tractorBeamImageView?.animationImages = imageArray.
compactMap { $0 }
tractorBeamImageView?.startAnimating()

if let tractorBeamImageView = tractorBeamImageView {
    view.insertSubview(tractorBeamImageView, at: 4)
}

let cowImageView = hitTest()

if let cowImageView = cowImageView {
    currentAbductee = cowImageView
    abductCow(cowImageView)
}
```

```
}
```

We first clear out the pointer to the current abducted cow. This
value should be nil already, but it is best to be diligent. We then set
a BOOL for whether the tractor beam is on to true/yes. At this point,
we need to draw the tractor beam. To do this, we set the frame for our
tractorBeamImageView to where the player's UFO is currently located.
We will be using the same animation shortcut that was demoed earlier in
this section to animate the tractor beam. We then add the tractor beam
imageView to the main view; we use an insertSubview function here to

make sure the tractor beam is below the cows but above the background. Then we call our hitTest function, which we will look at a little later in this chapter. If we get a result back from the hitTest, we call our abductCow function.

Before we can move on to the hitTest and abductCow functions, we must first finish handling our touch events. The only other touch event that we are concerned with at this point is the touchesEnded delegate call. When the user removes their finger from the screen, we want to remove the tractor beam from the view and let the user resume their movement.

```swift
override func touchesEnded(_ touches: Set<UITouch>, with event:
UIEvent?) {
        tractorBeamOn = false

        if gameIsMultiplayer {
            gcManager?.sendStringToAllPeers("$endTractorBeam",
            reliable: true)
        }

        tractorBeamImageView?.removeFromSuperview()

        if let currentAbductee = currentAbductee {
            UIView.animate(
                withDuration: 1.0,
                delay: 0,
                options: [.curveEaseIn, .beginFromCurrentState],
                animations: {
                    var frame = currentAbductee.frame

                    frame.origin.y = 260
                    frame.origin.x = (self.myPlayerImageView?.
                    frame.origin.x ?? 0.0) + 15
```

```
                    currentAbductee.frame = frame
            }
        )
    }

    currentAbductee = nil
}
```

Set the state variable for the `tractorBeamOn` to NO. Then we can remove the tractor beam image from the view. The next section of code drops the cow back to the ground (if there was one midway in the air). To do this, we just begin a simple animation where we return the cow to ground level. The last thing we need to do is reset the `currentAbductee` pointer to `nil`.

Spawning and Moving Cows

As mentioned earlier in this chapter, we also have a convenience function to spawn a new cow. This is the function we call from `viewDidLoad` to give the player a base number of cows to try and abduct; we also call this whenever we are finished abducting a cow.

```
func spawnCow() {
    let x = Int(arc4random() % 480)
    let cowImageView = UIImageView(frame: CGRect(x:
    CGFloat(x), y: 260, width: 64, height: 42))
    cowImageView.image = UIImage(named: "Cow1.png")
    view.addSubview(cowImageView)
    cowArray?.append(cowImageView)

}
```

Tip   Arc4Random() will return a random number the same way
that rand() or random() will but will automatically seed itself if it is
the first time it is being called.

We create a new imageView that will represent the cow. We then use an
arc4Random() function to produce a random x position. We set the image
that the cow will be using and add it to the main view. The last thing we
need to do here is add the imageView to our cow array. We will be using
this for a hit test as well as updating the movement paths.

While UFOs is not designed to be an extremely challenging game, we
do want to add at least some aspects of difficulty to the gameplay. The
following function will cause our cows to randomly wander around the
screen:

```
func updateCowPaths() {

        for x in 0..<(cowArray?.count ?? 0) {
        let tempCow = cowArray?[x] as? UIImageView

        if tempCow != currentAbductee && tempCow != otherPlayer
        CurrentAbductee {
                    let currentX = Float(tempCow?.frame.origin.x
                    ?? 0.0)
                    var newX = currentX + Float
                    (arc4random() % 100) - 50
        if newX > 480 {

            newX = 480
        }
        if newX < 0 {
            newX = 0
        }
```

```
if tempCow != currentAbductee {
    UIView.animate(
        withDuration: 3.0,
        delay: 0,
        options: [.curveLinear],
        animations: {
            tempCow?.frame = CGRect(x:
            CGFloat(newX), y: 260,
            width: 64, height: 42)
        }
    )
}

tempCow?.animationDuration = 0.75
tempCow?.animationRepeatCount = 99999

//flip cow
if newX < currentX {
    let flippedCowImageArray =
    [UIImage(named: "Cow1Reversed.png"),
    UIImage(named: "Cow2Reversed.png"),
    UIImage(named: "Cow3Reversed.png")]
    tempCow?.animationImages =
    flippedCowImageArray.compactMap { $0
    }
} else {
    let cowImageArray = [UIImage(named:
    "Cow1.png"), UIImage(named: "Cow2.
    png"), UIImage(named: "Cow3.png")]
    tempCow?.animationImages =
    cowImageArray.compactMap { $0 }
}
```

```
            tempCow?.startAnimating()

        }
    }

    //change the paths for the cows every 3 seconds
    DispatchQueue.main.asyncAfter(deadline: .now() +
    3, execute: {
        self.updateCowPaths()
    })
}
```

We will need to cycle through our array of cow objects. We do this on the first line of the preceding function. We then randomize a new x position for the cow. A quick check ensures we are not instructing the cow to walk off the screen. Then we commit the animation. We also need to handle the direction change for the cow.

Note   The code that we use to handle that event is not the most efficient manner of flipping an image, but it is the easiest to learn if you are new to this type of game.

As we had previously done with the tractor beam and the UFO images, we will add some animation frames so the cow walks more realistically. The last thing we do is call performSelector with a delay of three seconds. This will update the cow's path every three seconds, adding a more realistic appearance of random movement.

Performing a Hit Test with a UIImage

Before we can worry about how to set up the cow abduction, there are preliminary steps for abducting the cow itself. For starters, we must implement a hitTest function that was previously being called from the touchesBegan event that was discussed earlier in this section.

```swift
func hitTest() -> UIImageView? {
    if !tractorBeamOn {
        return nil
    }

    for x in 0..<(cowArray?.count ?? 0) {
        let tempCow = cowArray?[x] as? UIImageView
        let cowLayer = tempCow?.layer.presentation()
        let cowFrame = cowLayer?.frame

        if cowFrame?.intersects(tractorBeamImageView?.frame
        ?? CGRect.zero) ?? false {
            tempCow?.frame = cowLayer?.frame ?? CGRect.zero
            tempCow?.layer.removeAllAnimations()

            if gameIsMultiplayer {
                gcManager?.sendStringToAllPeers(String(for
                mat: "$abductCowAtIndex:%i", x), reliable:
                true)
            }

            return tempCow
        }
    }

    return nil
}
```

The first line is another sanity check to ensure that we are not calling the hitTest function when the tractorBeam is not on. Once we make sure we are supposed to be checking for the hit, we iterate through our array of cow objects. Since the cows are in the middle of an animation, we cannot rely on the data from the frame, as it will show where the cow will end up and not where the cow currently is.

To determine where the cow currently is, we ask for the presentationLayer. Core Graphics provides a useful function for testing whether two GCRects intersect, and that is what we will be using here. If we hit a cow, we return the object. If we get to the end of our loop without passing a hit test, we return nil, which lets us know that no cow was hit by the tractor beam.

Tip   presentationLayer can be called on any CALayer to provide a best guess on the current values of a layer that is currently in the process of being animated. While it does not absolutely guarantee the current position of the animation, it provides a good-enough solution for our game.

Abducting a Cow

In our touchesBegan function, we tested to see if hitTest returned a cow. If it did, we call abductCow with the object that was returned. We can now take a look at that function.

```
func abductCow(_ cowImageView: UIImageView?) {
    UIView.animate(
        withDuration: 4.0,
        delay: 0,
        options: [.curveEaseIn, .beginFromCurrentState],
```

```
        animations: {
            var frame = cowImageView?.frame
            frame?.origin.y = self.myPlayerImageView?.frame.
            origin.y ?? 0.0
            cowImageView?.frame = frame ?? CGRect.zero
        },
        completion: finishAbducting
    )
}
```

We begin an animation event on our cow object (which is an
imageView). We also set a completion handler, which will be called once
the animation has finished. We set the new y axis coordinate for the cow to
our UFO's current y axis coordinate and begin the animation.

Once the animation has stopped, we get a callback to
finishAbducting. This allows us to increase the score, clean up the
abducting code, and spawn a new cow.

```
func finishAbducting(_ finished: Bool) {
        if currentAbductee == nil || !tractorBeamOn {
            return
        }

        cowArray = cowArray?.filter({ ($0) as AnyObject !==
        (currentAbductee) as AnyObject })

        tractorBeamImageView?.removeFromSuperview()

        tractorBeamOn = false

        score += 1
        scoreLabel.text = String(format: "SCORE %05.0f", score)
```

```
currentAbductee?.layer.removeAllAnimations()
currentAbductee?.removeFromSuperview()

currentAbductee = nil

spawnCow()
}
```

At the beginning of the function, we check to see that the tractor beam is still on and that we have an abductee, once again just for some extra sanity and error checking. Just as we did when the user released their touch from the screen, we also want to remove the tractor beam image from the view and correctly set the state variables. We award the user with a single point for abducting each cow, and we update the scoreLabel accordingly. We clean up the old cow image and set it back to nil. Now we spawn a new cow to replace the abducted one.

Configuring App Store Connect for Game Center

Before your swift app or game can access any of the Game Center functionality, it will need to be configured in App Store Connect, formerly called iTunes Connect. Apple uses this portal as its main source for app configuration. Such functionality as in-app purchase (IAP), TestFlight, and Game Center requires App Store Connect configuration.

Note   You can still use any stand-alone GameKit functionality without setting up Game Center for your app. See Chapters 6, 7, 8, and 10 for more information on GameKit's stand-alone functionality.

Getting Started with App Store Connect

If you have never uploaded an app to the App Store, you might be unfamiliar with the App Store Connect portal. However, if you have worked with App Store Connect previously, you might want to skip to the next section, as this will be refresher for you.

App Store Connect is a web portal accessed from any web browser at `https://appstoreconnect.apple.com`. You will use your existing AppleID, which you registered as a developer with, to gain access to the portal. This is the same web application that you will use when you want to upload new apps for sale on the App Store, as well as make any changes to them, such as price or description. A view of the landing page for App Store Connect can be seen in Figure 1-4.

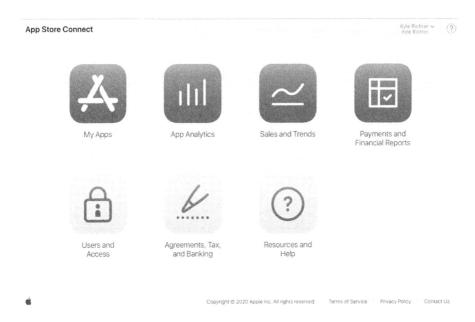

Figure 1-4. *A view of App Store Connect taken November 2020*

When you log in to App Store Connect, you will be presented with a wealth of options. The most important of these is setting up your contracts, tax, and banking information. While these requirements do not have anything to do with Game Center per se, it is good to get them out of the way.

It may take weeks for Apple to process this information, so submit it as soon as possible. Until this information is processed and approved, you will be unable to release software on the App Store. Once you have completed all the requested information under this section, you can focus on the app development itself.

Note   If you plan on releasing only free apps, you do not need to complete the paid apps contracts. However, if you plan on releasing any paid software in the future, these should be completed as soon as possible.

Before you can access any Game Center–specific information, you will need to create a new (or use an existing) app. This is a straightforward process that you will be walked through in App Store Connect. You begin under the My Apps section; there you will find a small plus button near the web page title in the upper left corner. The rest should be fairly self-explanatory.

If you are not yet ready to upload an app, you can create placeholder data here to gain access to the Game Center portal. Once your app has been created in App Store Connect, you can begin to configure the Game Center–specific information.

Caution   If you create an app and fail to upload a release build within 90 days, Apple will delete the app information and restrict you from creating a new app with the same name in the future. This is an effort to prevent people from "domain squatting" app names.

Configuring Game Center in App Store Connect

Once you have selected your app from within App Store Connect, you will see a view similar to the screen capture in Figure 1-5, shown later in this section. If you direct your attention to navigation bar, you will notice a features item; this is where Game Center items will be configured.

If you are familiar with in-app purchase in previous apps, this area will seem very familiar to you. The process for configuring IAP is similar to working with Game Center.

Once you navigate to the features area for the app, you will be given an option to add challenges, new leaderboards, or achievements. We focus on these options more in later chapters (Chapter 3 covers leaderboards, and Chapter 4 covers achievements). For now, all we need to do is ensure that our app is set up and ready for Game center functionality to be added.

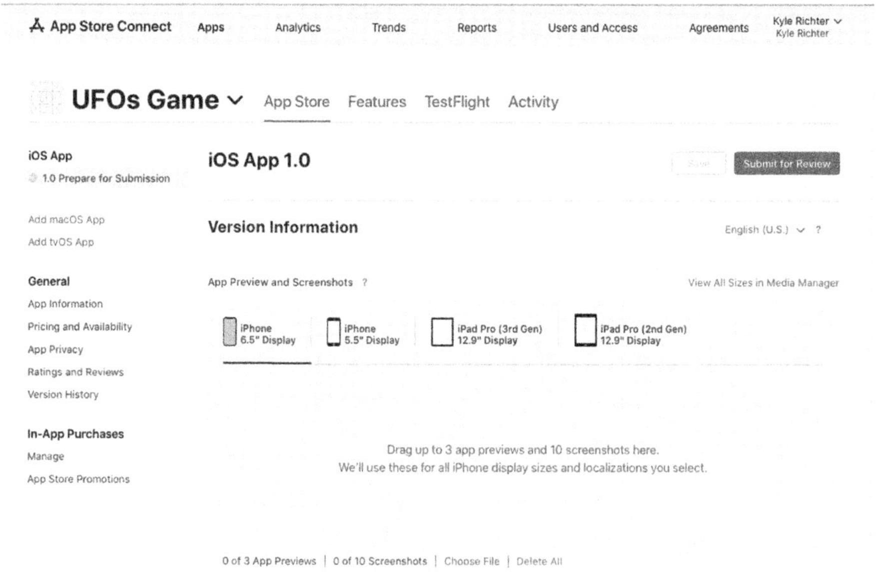

Figure 1-5. *The first view of the Game Center portal for a new App*

Make sure to check off the Game Center functionality under the General App Information on the first tab ("App Store" on your new app), otherwise your App may not register as having Game Center functionality.

Tip   If you are having difficulty getting your app to acknowledge Game Center, the most likely culprit is one of two common issues. Make sure your app is using the same bundle ID that is shown in the App Info page. The second issue may be that you have not let enough time pass. There can be up to a 30-minute delay between making changes in App Store Connect to Game Center and having the app notice those changes.

Summary

You should now have a basic understanding of what GameKit and Game Center have to offer, as well as an in-depth understanding of the sample project you will be working with throughout the course of this book. Additionally, you should now be comfortable setting up a new app in App Store Connect for use with Game Center.

In the upcoming chapters, you will learn how to incorporate all the functionality of Game Center and GameKit into an app. In the next chapter, you will learn how to get Game Center incorporated into a project.

CHAPTER 2

Game Center: Configuring and Getting Started

In the last chapter, we learned how to configure Game Center in App Store Connect and began working with the sample project, UFOs. In this chapter, we will discuss integrating Game Center into our app and get our hands dirty with some code.

You will learn how to detect Game Center compatibility, explore the limitations of the sandbox, authenticate a local player, work with sessions, and retrieve a friends list. You will also create the Game Center Manager class that we will be working with and expanding throughout the rest of the book.

Creating a Game Center Manager Class

When Game Center was first released, it was important to test for compatibility before implementing it; however, Game Center has readily been available across all our platforms for years, and unless you plan on targeting very old devices, there is no longer a need to make sure a device is running it. On our way to implementing Game Center functionality,

© Kyle Richter and Beau G. Bolle 2022
K. Richter and B. G. Bolle, *Beginning iOS Game Center and GameKit*,
https://doi.org/10.1007/978-1-4842-7756-0_2

the first thing we need to do to perform this check is to create our new GameCenterManager class. We will use this class throughout the remainder of this book to keep our Game Center functionality in one easy-to-access class. This class will house all of our Game Center–specific code and callbacks and can be easily shared and reused across all of your apps.

First, create a new Swift file in Xcode; name the new class GameCenterManager, as shown in Figure 2-1. You will also want to add the GameKit.framework to your project at this time, as well as add the import GameKit line to the top of the newly created GameCenterManager class.

Figure 2-1. *Creating the GameCenterManager Class*

Authenticating with Game Center

Before doing anything with Game Center, you first need to authenticate the user. The user who is authenticated with Game Center will always be referred to as the local player and will be represented by the class GKLocalPlayer. Failing to authenticate a local user before making calls to other Game Center functionality will result in errors and other undefined behaviors.

Apple recommends that you authenticate with Game Center as early as possible in your app. The primary reason to authenticate before the user needs to access any Game Center behavior is to ensure that the user is not waiting for the network callbacks to authenticate a user at a time when they want to perform a Game Center action. Early authentication also makes sure that the user is not prompted for a login in the middle of gameplay, which would detract from the user experience. There are additional benefits of authenticating before the user may need to that we will explore in upcoming chapters, such as resubmitting high scores that failed to submit at an earlier time.

Modifying the GameCenterManager Class

Handling authentication requires additional code to the GameCenterManager class. This is done by expanding on the GameCenterManager struct. The first step is to define a new function to handle the authentication; we will call this authenticateLocalUser. A completion handler is defined as the calling view controller; this will allow us to report errors and successes back to the main game. Next, a quick sanity check is done to make sure that the local player authentication handler isn't already defined, and then define it as the calling view controller.

```swift
class GameCenterManager: UIViewController,
GKMatchmakerViewControllerDelegate, GKLocalPlayerListener,
UIAlertViewDelegate {
    func authenticateLocalUser(_ controller: UIViewController?) {
        let localPlayer = GKLocalPlayer.local
        if localPlayer.isAuthenticated == false {
            localPlayer.authenticateHandler = { [weak self]
            viewController, error in
                guard let self = self else {
                    return
                }
                if let viewController = viewController {
                    controller?.present(viewController,
                    animated: true)
                }
                if localPlayer.isAuthenticated {
                    localPlayer.unregisterListener(self)
                    self.submitAllSavedScores()
                    self.submitAllSavedAchievements()
                    DispatchQueue.main.asyncAfter(deadline:
                    .now() + 3) { [weak self] in
                        self?.populateAchievementCache(nil)
                    }
                    GKLocalPlayer.local.register(self)
                }
                self.playerDelegate?.processGameCenter
                Authentication(error)
            }
        }
    }
```

Tip   Don't forget to import the GameKit framework, otherwise, GKLocalPlayer will be undefined.

Authenticating from UFOViewController

The preceding function will serve as a helper for authenticating with Game Center. While the Game Center Manager code has been configured to log the player in, your app needs to call this new function. You will need to swift your attention back to the HomeViewController, which is the view controller that the game launches to, before any gameplay begins. The following code can be added into the viewDidLoad function:

```swift
func authenticateLocalUser(_ controller: UIViewController?) {
    let localPlayer = GKLocalPlayer.local
    if localPlayer.isAuthenticated == false {
        localPlayer.authenticateHandler = { [weak self]
        viewController, error in
            guard let self = self else {
                return
            }
            if let viewController = viewController {
                controller?.present(viewController, animated:
                true)
            }
            if localPlayer.isAuthenticated {
                localPlayer.unregisterListener(self)
                self.submitAllSavedScores()
                self.submitAllSavedAchievements()
                DispatchQueue.main.asyncAfter(deadline:
                .now() + 3) { [weak self] in
```

```
                self?.populateAchievementCache(nil)
            }
            GKLocalPlayer.local.register(self)
        }
        self.playerDelegate?.processGameCenter
        Authentication(error)
    }
  }
}
```

The first line of code calls the authenticateLocalUser function from the Game Center Manager. After that, an error check is performed before the login view controller is shown. In the event that an error is encountered, we present the user with an alert window letting them know about the error. If there was no error, then the Game Center Login screen is presented.

Game Center handles the required login views and authentication as well as any account creation at this point. However, we do need to watch our authentication completion handler in order to catch any errors encountered while authenticating.

Caution   If you have cancelled a Game Center login three or more times from within an app, you will not be able to sign in from that app again until you have gone to the GameCenter.app and signed in. This is an undocumented behavior and can be a real pain to trace if you do not know what you are searching for. In addition, if you find you are unable to sign in even from Game Center.app, you can reset the simulator or restore the device to resolve these issues. It is rare for a user of your app to face these issues, but as a developer, the constant debugging and error testing more often than not will put you into an expected behavioral state.

Tip   If you encounter the error "This game is not recognized by Game Center," make sure to check your bundle identifier and that it matches the app that you set up in App Store Connect.

It is important here to take a few moments to talk about thread safety. Thread safety may be a term you are very familiar with, might be something you have heard briefly touched on in our materials, or may even be a completely new term for you. While it is beyond the scope of this book to dive too deeply into threads, it's important to at least have a cursory understanding of the technology.

When an app executes and runs, it can do so in sequence along a single thread, meaning that the next task will not begin until the previous task has finished. This is called synchronous execution. On the other hand, you can have multiple tasks all running at the same time and finishing in whatever order they happen to finish; this is called asynchronous. Running code asynchronously is often faster because modern devices have multiple cores which can each handle one or more tasks at a time. However not knowing when tasks will finish running, having tasks finish before other tasks, or trying to have two tasks modify the same object at once can result in bugs, unexpected behavior, and even hard-to-track-down race conditions.

You may have noticed that when reviewing sample codes, frameworks, methods, or functions, the author will sometimes denote whether something is thread safe, isn't thread safe, or needs to be executed on the main thread. These notations will allow you to make smart decisions on how to write the most optimal code and guide you through avoiding bugs and crashes. As a general rule of thumb, if you are updating an interface item, such as displaying a button, launching an alert, or changing the color of something on the screen, that action must be done on the main thread.

Many of the features of Game Center and GameKit will require the execution of the code on the main thread. Since we are not running the authentication of the local user on a background thread, there are not any changes that we need to make in the sample app. However, if you are designing an app that will be authenticating from a background thread, make sure to access the authentication function through a main thread; while there are numerous ways to accomplish this, the easiest, albeit perhaps not the most optimal, is as follows:

```
DispatchQueue.main.async { [unowned self] in
    self.yourCodeHere()
}
```

While your app should continue to function normally whether or not a user has signed into Game Center, it may be necessary to set some flags or perform some other actions upon successful login.

You can add the following code snippet to the end of the authenticateLocalUser completion handler:

```
if (GKLocalPlayer.local.isAuthenticated)
{
    print("Successfully authenticated")
}
```

Now when you log in, you should see "Successfully authenticated" printed to the console, as well as the image shown in Figure 2-2 (with your Game Center name instead).

Caution   When logging in to Game Center for testing purposes, always create a new Apple ID. Never use an existing Apple ID to log in to Game Center from the sandbox environment. There have been historic incidents where a user account can become broken during testing, and it can be a huge hassle to deal with a broken account on your primary Apple ID.

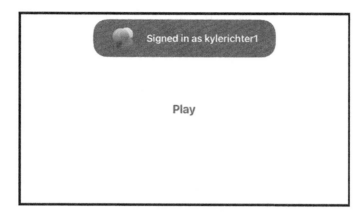

Figure 2-2. *The standard welcome back message the user will see when logging in to Game Center*

Tip   If you are having trouble logging in, make sure your bundle ID in the info.plist matches a bundle ID that has Game Center enabled for it in App Store Connect. See Chapter 1 for more information on configuring Game Center in App Store Connect.

Watching for Status Changes

With multiple apps running in the background and depending on the device side by side, the authentication can become a little more complex, with a user logging in and out through different apps. For example, the user may log out of Game Center, or even log in as a different user, while your app is in the background. Therefore, it is vital that you listen for changes to the local user through the NSNotification system.

Add the following snippet of code in viewDidLoad of UFOViewController.m right after the test is performed to verify whether Game Center is available:

```
NotificationCenter.default.addObserver(self, selector:
#selector(localUserAuthenticationChanged(_:)), name:
NSNotification.Name.GKPlayerAuthentication
DidChangeNotificationName, object: nil)
```

You also want to add a new function to UFOViewController. This function will be called whenever player authentication status changes.

```
@objc private func localUserAuthenticationChanged(_
notification: Notification) {
    print("Authentication changed: \(notification.object ??
    "()")")
    }
```

This new function will print the description for the new GKLocalPlayer when authentication changes. You will need to determine what special steps need to be taken in your app to handle local player changes.

Tip   Do not forget to test user switching before shipping your app, as Apple will test it in the review stage.

Working with GKLocalPlayer

The GKLocalPlayer will always exist and be non-nil when authenticated with Game Center; this object is a representation of the user. You will never create an instance of GKLocalPlayer; this is handled through the class method localPlayer. The localPlayer singleton will be the only way that you will interact with the localPlayer.

The GKLocalPlayer has several properties associated with it: authenticated, underage, isMultiplayerGamingRestricted, and isPersonalizedCommunicationRestricted. We will be dealing with the friends property in the following section. We have already worked with the authenticated Boolean in our authentication code in the previous sections.

The underage, isMultiplayerGamingRestricted, and isPersonalizedCommunicationRestricted properties are useful for restricting content in a Game Center–enabled app. The following code performs an underage check; similar code can be added for multiplayer or communication restrictions:

```
if (GKLocalPlayer.local.isUnderage)
{
    print("User is Underage")
}
```

Game Center Friends

When Game Center was first released, a lot of focus was placed on building and managing your personal friends list. Over the years this has become less of a priority and focus for Apple. The friends property of the local user was deprecated in iOS 8 and replaced with a loadFriendPlayers which was in turn deprecated in iOS 10. Finally, loadRecentPlayers was introduced and remains usable in iOS 14. You may notice that this function doesn't include the language "friends"; however, the documentation provides more insight. Asynchronously load the challengeable friends list as an array of GKPlayer. A challengeable player is a player with friend levels 1 and 2, or FL1 and FL2. This function calls a completionHandler when finished. The error will be nil on success. The Game Center controls in the settings app still lets you add friends.

While having playable friends continues to be deprioritized in new updates to Game Center, the functionality does remain to get a list of GKPlayers that are friends to the authenticated local user.

In order to retrieve a list of all of your existing Game Center friends, the following function may be utilized:

```
func retrieveFriendsList() {
    if GKLocalPlayer.local.isAuthenticated == true {
        GKLocalPlayer.local.loadRecentPlayers(completionHandler:
        { [weak self] recentPlayers, error in
            DispatchQueue.main.async { [weak self] in
                self?.playerDelegate?.friendsFinishedLoading(
                recentPlayers, error: error)
            }
        })
    } else {
        print("You must authenicate first")
    }
}
```

This method will call back to friendsFinishedLoading when the data has been fully retrieved. In the following code snippet, you can see an implementation of what that function might look like:

```
func friendsFinishedLoading(_ friends: [GKPlayer]?, error:
Error?) {
        if let error = error {
            print("An error occured during friends list
            request: \(error.localizedDescription)")
        } else if let friends = friends {
            playerDataLoaded(friends, error: error)
        }
    }
```

Once the data has been loaded from the server, a final function is implemented to print that data to the console.

```
func playerDataLoaded(_ players: [GKPlayer]?, error: Error?) {
    if let error = error {
        print("An error occured during player lookup: \(error.
        localizedDescription)")
    } else {
        print("Players loaded: \(players ?? [])")
    }
}
```

Working with Players

At the heart of Game Center is a social service, and as such, it revolves around players be it challenges, multiplayer, leaderboards, or competing for achievements. You need to be aware of properties associated with a GKPlayer object. Three properties handle the name of the player, gamePlayerID, and teamPlayerID, which are unique identifiers that will refer to a player. The gamePlayerID is static and will always point to the same player for the same game, while teamPlayerID is unique to the player across all games from your developer account. The teamPlayerID therefore allows you to identify a player across multiple apps and can be very powerful for marketing and cross-promotion. The gamePlayerID and teamPlayerID string should never be shown to the user in your app; it is used purely for internal reference. The alias or displayName, on the other hand, is dynamic and can be changed by the user at any time. A Game Center user can set a new alias at any time; the alias property will always display the alias; if you use displayName, it will always display the alias unless a user is a friend, and then it will show their real names instead. The alias and displayName should never be used to test the identity of a user, but they should be the only string used to identify the player to your app's user. It is important to also keep in mind that an alias is not unique and more than one player may have identical aliases or displayNames.

Caution   Do not make assumptions about the structure of the player identifier string. Its format and length are subject to change.

When looking at any list of player IDs in Game Center, we do not begin with GKPlayer objects, instead we have an array of user IDs. To help us work with players, we will add two additional convenience methods to translate player IDs into GKPlayers objects.

We need to create two new functions: one will handle an array of player IDs, and the other will handle a single player ID. This will save us extra work down the road. We add the helper methods to our GameCenterManager class.

We will add the following two function methods to the GameCenterManager class:

```
func playersForIDs(_ playerIDs: [String]) {
      GKPlayer.loadPlayers(forIdentifiers: playerIDs) {
      [weak self] players, error in
          DispatchQueue.main.async {
              self?.playerDelegate?.playerDataLoaded(players,
              error: error)
          }
      }
  }
  func playerForID(_ playerID: String) {
      playersForIDs([playerID])
        }
```

Now, when the App is run (assuming you have friends associated with your Game Center account), it will pull down a list of your friends' player

IDs and then perform a lookup and print the GKPlayer description to the console. Your output should look similar to the following:

```
UFOs[4038:207] Authentication Changed: <GKPlayer-
0x5f46fb0>(playerID: G:1092793231, alias: the_other_kyle,
status: (null), rid:(null)) UFOs[4038:207] Players loaded:
("<GKPlayer 0x6a201e0>(playerID: G:1093075676, alias: johncash,
status: (null),4-rid:(null))"
)
```

Summary

In this chapter, you learned how to test for Game Center compatibility and authenticate the local user. You should now have a strong grasp of how we will be using the Game Center Manager class and the benefits it will have on creating a clean code environment that will be easily reusable across multiple projects.

In the next chapter, we will take an in-depth look at leaderboards and expand on topics learned in this chapter. If you have any difficulty with anything discussed in this chapter, remember that the included sample code contains working examples of all the topics discussed.

CHAPTER 3

Leaderboards

Leaderboards are older than video games themselves. The leaderboard, as we know it, goes back to the days of the original pinball games of the 1950s. The makers of these pinball games soon realized that adding a high-score list increased competition, which translates to more time played and more money earned.

During the 1970s, when video games began to emerge, leaderboards were quickly adopted into these new games, making their first appearance in Sea Wolf, released in 1976 (see Figure 3-1). Since then, they have played an integral part of the gaming culture. Leaderboards have become so widespread that, in 2007, *The King of Kong*, a full-length documentary, was released about the heated competition over the high score on Nintendo's Donkey Kong. *The King of Kong* was so popular that it even led to a musical titled *King of Kong: The Musical* and a rumored scripted film adaptation is in the works by director Seth Gordon. Leaderboards have become so mainstream that they are now an expected part of any video game. They remain one of the easiest ways to build in completeness and replayability to a game.

© Kyle Richter and Beau G. Bolle 2022
K. Richter and B. G. Bolle, *Beginning iOS Game Center and GameKit*,
https://doi.org/10.1007/978-1-4842-7756-0_3

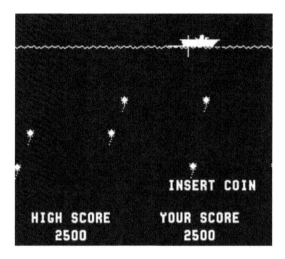

Figure 3-1. *Sea Wolf (1976), the first video game to feature a high score*

Game Center for iOS, Mac, and Apple TV greatly simplifies adding leaderboards to your project. This is a huge improvement when you consider that, previously, a developer had to write and maintain a server to hold, push, and retrieve the scores from. In this chapter, we examine the steps required to implement multiple leaderboards under Game Center, as well as all the required leaderboard support. You learn how to post scores, retrieve leaderboards, customize the graphical user interface (GUI) of leaderboards, and everything else needed to create leaderboards that are the right fit for your app.

Why a Leaderboard?

Before we get into working with leaderboards themselves, it is important to understand why leaderboards are an integral part of your social app or game:

- Leaderboards create a sense of community in an app or game that, otherwise, might not allow your user to interact directly with other users.

- Leaderboards drive users to return to your app in an effort to beat their own, their friends, or the community at large scores.

- Leaderboards create a sense of goal and accomplishment in an app.

- Leaderboards make it easier for users to share their app experience and progress with their friends, family, and peers.

- Leaderboards in Game Center are easy to implement and can make your app quickly feel more polished and finished.

An Overview of Leaderboards in Game Center

A leaderboard, in the sense of Game Center, is an array of GKScore objects related to a specific leaderboard identifier, of which many can exist per app. Leaderboards can be retrieved and further filtered based on friend status and date submitted.

GKScore objects represent each entry on a specific leaderboard. A GKScore always has a player ID associated with it. When submitting a new GKScore to a leaderboard, the player ID is set automatically by the API and cannot be changed. There are also values for the date and rank that are automatically set and updated. You are required to set only the raw score value and leaderboard category to which the score belongs.

There are two ways to retrieve and display leaderboards. The most common, and easiest, method is by using Apple's leaderboard GUI. This will be the first approach we learn about in the following sections. The second option is to retrieve the raw GKScore values and display them in your own GUI; this method is also discussed later in this chapter.

47

Leaderboard sets were introduced in iOS 7; these sets allow the developer to combine several leaders together into a single group. Leaderboard sets are flexible and may be used in many different ways, the most popular is to have groups of leaderboards for different worlds or difficulties in your game. You can define up to 100 leaderboard sets each containing up to 100 leaderboards.

Note   Game Center currently has a limit of 100 leaderboards or leaderboard sets per bundle ID. When you work with Leaderboard sets, the leaderboard limit is increased to 500 while still respecting the 100 leaderboards per leaderboard set limit. .

Benefits of Using Apple's Leaderboard GUI vs. a Custom GUI

Benefits of using Apple's leaderboard GUI include the following:

- The design was created by some of the best designers in the world. When Apple updates the designs, they will automatically be updated in your App, giving your user interface an instant facelift and keeping it feeling more modern, even if you haven't been regularly updating.

- It is very simple to implement and present the leaderboard.

- Users will see a familiar interface that they already know how to interact with.

Benefits of using a custom GUI include the following:

- Your leaderboard can match the custom design of your app.

- You have more freedom over the resulting data and can filter using additional criteria.

- You can implement your own custom caching behavior.

As you can see, there are advantages and disadvantages of each system, and there is no right answer in which one you should be using. At the end of this chapter, you will have a strong background in both options and will be able to make the correct decision on which method to implement based on the specific needs of your app.

Configuring a Leaderboard in App Store Connect

Before working with the code side of leaderboards, you must first set up a new leaderboard in App Store Connect. Log in to App Store Connect (https://appstoreconnect.apple.com/), and select the app that we have already been working with from Chapters 1 and 2. Once you have selected your app from the control panel, go to the Features area, and then select Game Center.

The Game Center portal for your app will have a section labeled "Leaderboards." Once you are in the leaderboard section (see Figure 3-2), select the "+" button in the upper left-hand corner of the leaderboard section. You will be prompted to select either a Classic Leaderboard or a Recurring Leaderboard. A Classic Leaderboard will build a list of scores which are permeant to your game and will never reset. Alternatively, a Recurring Leaderboard will have a fixed amount of time specified that the leaderboard will automatically reset, such as weekly.

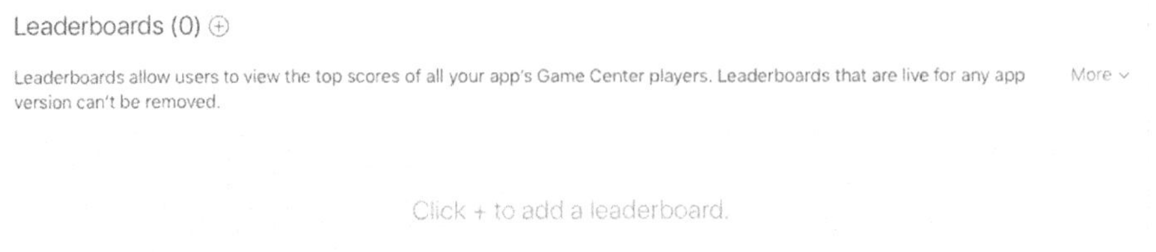

Leaderboards (0) ⊕

Leaderboards allow users to view the top scores of all your app's Game Center players. Leaderboards that are live for any app   More ∨
version can't be removed.

Click + to add a leaderboard.

Figure 3-2. *Adding a new leaderboard in App Store Connect*

We begin by creating a new classic leaderboard, as shown in Figure 3-3. The first thing you need to enter is the Leaderboard Reference Name. This value is used solely as a reference within App Store Connect. The reference name is designed to help you quickly find leaderboards within App Store Connect; the user never sees it. For this example, you can use the reference name "Leaderboard Foo."

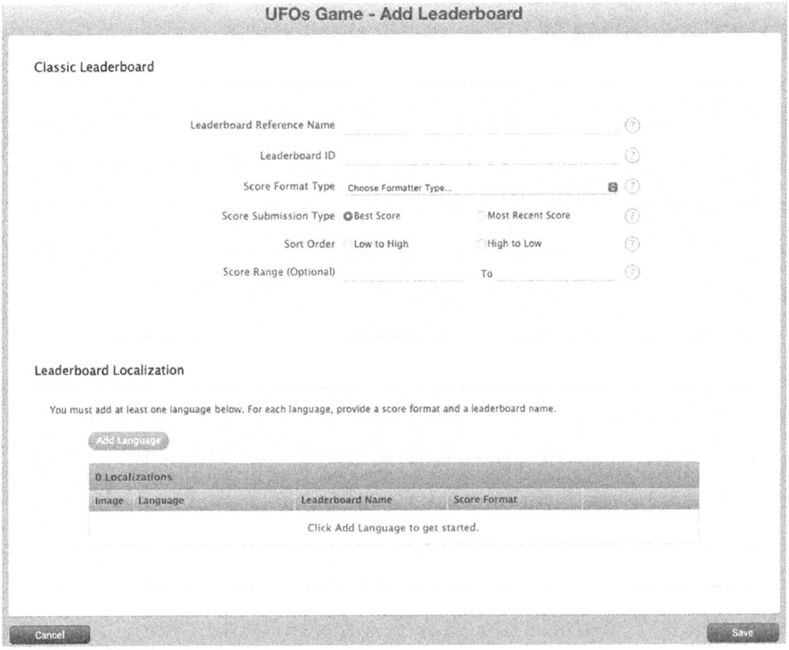

Figure 3-3. *Creating a new classic leaderboard in App Store Connect*

The next field is the Leaderboard ID, the value you will query in your code to retrieve a particular leaderboard. Apple recommends that you use a reverse DNS-type entry for this field, such as com.company.appname. leaderboardname. Fill in the appropriate values for your app here; it is not important what they are, but you will need to remember them throughout the remainder of this chapter.

The score format type is also required when creating a new leaderboard. Select the score format that meets the requirements for your score data. For information on score data formats, see Table 3-1.

Table 3-1. *Score Format Types for Adding a New Leaderboard in App Store Connect*

Score Format Type	Example Output
Integer	12,345
Fixed point, to 1 decimal	12,345.1
Fixed point, to 2 decimals	12,345.12
Fixed point, to 3 decimals	12,345.123
Elapsed time, to the minute	3:45
Elapsed time, to the second	3:45:55
Elapsed time, to the hundredth of a Second	3:45:55.82
Money, whole numbers	$182,121
Money, to 2 decimals	$182,121.68

Tip   If none of the provided format types match your requirements, select the one that best matches your needs. Later in this chapter, you will see how to customize these values by retrieving the raw score values.

The next field is for the Score Submission Type; there are two options available: Best Score and Most Recent Score. Select Best Score if you want the best score displayed first. Select Most Recent Score if you want the most recent score displayed first.

You also need to select whether you want the leaderboard to sort by ascending or descending order. Ascending order will display the lowest score first, as in a golf game or a lap around a track. Descending order will show the highest scores first, as in a game of football or a typical score in a first-person shooter.

There is also an optional score range field. This prevents users from submitting scores outside of the approved range; for example, if you have a golf game, you can't reasonably expect someone to submit a score of under 18 for an 18-hole game; likewise you probably don't want someone to be able to submit a score of 100,000. This field is optional but can prevent out-of-whack leaderboard caused by mischievous user behavior.

The last thing that needs to be done when creating a new classic leaderboard is entering the localized score information, as shown in Figure 3-4. App Store Connect contains built-in localization support for Game Center; you will need to create a new entry for each language you want to support. You can also add a unique image to be displayed along with your localized leaderboard.

The Name field is the display name for your leaderboard in the chosen language. The Score Format field will vary depending on the score format type you selected on the previous screen. (See Figure 3-4 for an example of money formatting.) You also need to provide a score format suffix. This string will be appended to the end of your score value when retrieving the formatted score property.

Caution   You will need to add at least one language for every leaderboard you create before it can be considered valid.

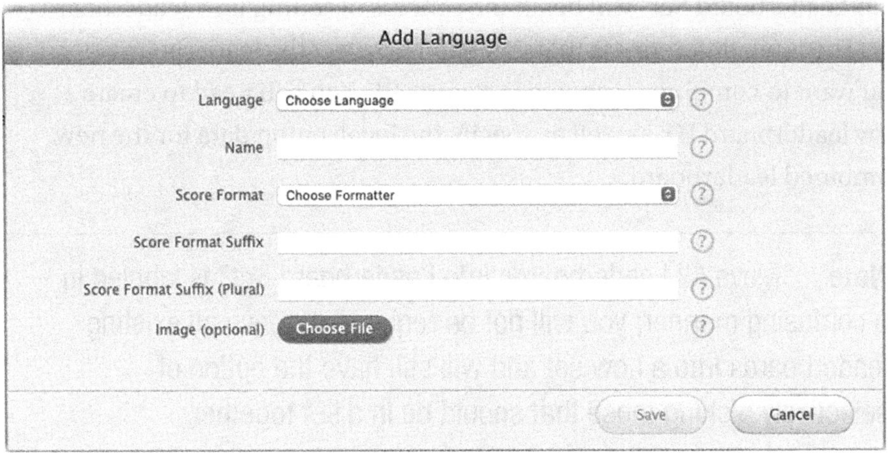

Add Language

Language	Choose Language
Name	
Score Format	Choose Formatter
Score Format Suffix	
Score Format Suffix (Plural)	
Image (optional)	Choose File

Save   Cancel

Figure 3-4. *Editing the localization information on a new leaderboard*

Tip   If you want a space to appear between the score and the score format suffix in the formatted score value, don't forget to add a space before the beginning of the score suffix.

You now have a classic leaderboard configured for your app. There may be situations in which you want to create a leaderboard set, or a group of leaderboards that have a common attribute. For example, your game has several different worlds with each world containing several leaderboards for most coins collected, highest score obtained, and most enemies killed. In order to enable a leaderboard set, we need at least two leaderboards that share the same type of score format. Go ahead and create a second classic leaderboard now.

Once you have two leaderboards that share the same score format type, you can create a leaderboard set. Once you have two leaderboards created, an option labeled "More" will appear at the top right portion of the Leaderboard interface section. The option "Move All Leaderboards

Into Leaderboard Set" will begin the process of setting up a leaderboard set. The main difference is that you need to select the leaderboards you want to combine, as shown in Figure 3-5. You will need to create a new leaderboard ID, as well as specify the localization data for the new combined leaderboard.

Note   "Move All Leaderboards Into Leaderboard Set" is labeled in a confusing manner; you will not be required to move all existing leaderboards into a new set and will still have the option of selectively picking those that should be in a set together.

Move Leaderboards Into Sets

Leaderboard Sets [Edit] [Delete]

Leaderboard Set   Test Set (com.ufo.dfsw.leaderboardset)   ⊟

These leaderboards will be available for display in Game Center. You must add at least one leaderboard.
[Add Leaderboard Set]

Leaderboards in This Set

These leaderboards will be available for display in Game Center. You must add at least one leaderboard.
[Add to Leaderboard Set]

0 Leaderboards

Reference Name	Leaderboard ID	Localizations
You don't have any leaderboards in this leaderboard set. To get started, click Add to Leaderboard Set.		

Figure 3-5. *Creating a combined leaderboard*

We will also add one last single leaderboard to let us work with a single uncombined leaderboard, as the two previous leaderboards that we had created are now "Attached"-type leaderboards. Your leaderboard panel should now have four leaderboards in it: two attached, one combined, and one single leaderboard. Now that we have a handful of valid leaderboards to work with, we can move back to Xcode and begin to work with the leaderboard-specific code.

Important   Once a leaderboard has gone live in a shipping app, it can never be removed, so double-check your leaderboard information before shipping an app.

Recurring Leaderboards

Apple has recently expanded the capabilities of leaderboards to allow time-limited leaderboards, referred to as recurring leaderboards. These are added just like a classic leaderboard, except the option for recurring is selected when prompted. A recurring leaderboard will feature three new options. The first is the date and time that the leaderboard will first become available to the user, the second is a duration that the leaderboard will be available for, and finally a delay for the leaderboard to reset and become available again. Referring to Figure 3-6, a new leaderboard will appear beginning June 7, 2021, and will collect scores for 24 hours; every 7 days the leaderboard will reset all of its scores and become available for another 24-hour period.

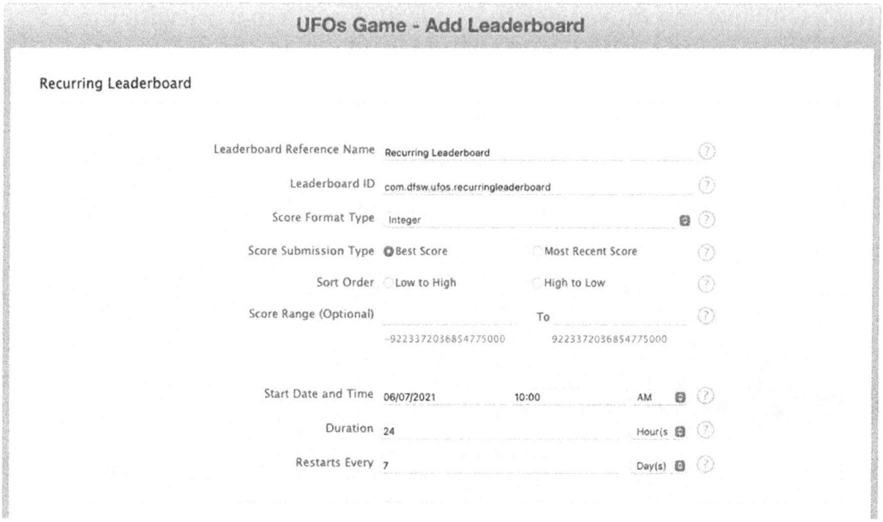

UFOs Game - Add Leaderboard

Recurring Leaderboard

Leaderboard Reference Name	Recurring Leaderboard
Leaderboard ID	com.dfsw.ufos.recurringleaderboard
Score Format Type	Integer
Score Submission Type	○ Best Score ○ Most Recent Score
Sort Order	○ Low to High ○ High to Low
Score Range (Optional)	To
	-9223372036854775000 9223372036854775000
Start Date and Time	06/07/2021 10:00 AM
Duration	24 Hour(s)
Restarts Every	7 Day(s)

Figure 3-6.   Creating a recurring leaderboard

Posting a Score

Before a leaderboard provides any useful functionality, we need to populate it with some score data. We begin this process by modifying our GameCenterManager class once again. Add the following function to the implementation; it should look very familiar as it follows the same pattern that we used when we implemented the authentication methods:

```
func reportScore(_ score: Int, forCategory category: String) {
    GKLeaderboard.submitScore(score, context: 0, player:
    GKLocalPlayer.local, leaderboardIDs: [category]) { [weak
    self] error in
        if let error = error {
            print("An error occurred while submitting a score.
            Data will be saved to UserDefaults:
            \(error.localizedDescription)")
```

```
        let savedScore = SavedScore(score: score, category:
        category)
        self?.storeScoreForLater(savedScore)
    }
    DispatchQueue.main.async { [weak self] in
        self?.gameDelegate?.scoreReported(error)
    }
  }
}
```

This new method takes an integer for the score and a GKLeaderboard object. The date and user values are already set for us by the API. When submitScore is called on the GKLeaderboard, it accepts the score, a player context, and the player that is submitting the score, which should always be the local player.

This concludes all of the required modifications to our GameCenterManager class. We can now turn our focus back to the game itself. We will need to first implement some new gameplay dynamics to handle high scores.

Adding Score Posting to UFOs

There are two obvious ways that we can score in our UFOs game. Firstly, we could implement a system that counted how many cows were abducted and submit that as the score. Although this approach is the easiest to implement for us, it is not a very fun gameplay technique because there is no logical point at which the game ends. Secondly, high-score method is harder to implement but makes more sense. It clocks how long the user took to abduct ten cows; the user with the lowest time is the winner.

These are topics that must be carefully considered for your own app; sometimes the most straightforward approach to high scores isn't the most fun for the user. For the purpose of this book, we will demonstrate the first method in which the number of cows abducted is the user's score. If you were going to implement a timer-based system, the approach is very similar: you would start a timer at the beginning of the round, and when ten cows are abducted, you would submit the time in seconds on the timer.

In order to implement this score-based system, we need to add a way for the player to end a game. In an actual game, this could be handled by something being able to kill your player, or a time limit. However, for the purpose of this example, we will simply add an exit button. This will allow the user to simulate a game-over event while keeping the code Game Center–focused without adding extra complexity.

We add an exit button in UFOGameViewController.xib, as shown in Figure 3-7. We will need to create a new IBAction for the exit button as well. Add the following code to UFOGameViewController, and connect our exit button to it. For the time being, we will just pop the navigation controller back to the root view:

```
@IBAction func exitAction(_ sender: Any) {
    navigationController?.popViewController(animated: true)
}
```

Note   You are not required to wait until the end of a game to submit a new score, but it is generally thought of as good practice. You want to avoid submitting a new score multiple times per game if it can be prevented.

A notable exception might be a continuous role-playing game in which the score continually updates, and there is no proper ending to submit a score during the game.

Figure 3-7. *Adding the ability to exit the game so a high score can be submitted*

The only remaining step is to actually submit the score to Game Center; if you recall, we have already written the method to handle this in our GameCenterManager class. We already have an instance of our GameCenterManager class that we used in UFOViewController to authenticate the user.

We will also modify the exitAction method to just submit the score. To do so, replace the old exitAction function with the following. Notice how we are using the leaderboard ID that we set in App Store Connect; make sure to use the same one that you entered, as it will probably not match this example:

```
@IBAction func exitAction(_ sender: Any) {
    navigationController?.popViewController(animated: true)
    gcManager?.reportScore(Int64(score), forCategory:
    "com.dragonforged.ufo.single")
}
```

59

When you now play and click Exit, you should see a console message that looks similar to the following output:

```
2011-02-10 12:32:47.629 UFOs[15092:207] Score submitted
```

Tip   See the section, "A Better Approach," at the end of this chapter for a more complex, but user-friendly, approach to submitting scores.

Now that we have a score submitted to a leaderboard, in the following sections, we will learn how to present this data back to the user. This action has been greatly simplified for the purpose of making this section as easy to learn as possible. This will not be the user experience you want to present to your user; we are simply trapping the user in the game screen while we wait for a network callback. In reality, you will want to handle the delegate callback in the previous view. This ensures the user is not waiting when they do not have to be. For simplicity's sake, we will continue to use the easier-to-follow methodology.

Tip   You can only have one score posted per leaderboard category for each player. You might notice that the scores that you are submitting never appear on the leaderboard. If you are noticing this behavior, make sure that the score you are submitting is higher than the highest score for that player.

Handling Failures When Submitting a Score

If a score fails to submit, you as the developer are solely responsible for storing the score and resubmitting it when the error has been resolved. Nothing is more frustrating to a user than earning a new high score and losing it due to a network failure or even a crash. This is also a step that Apple likes to test for during app reviews, so keep in mind you may have a rejection if you fail to implement it properly.

There are many different ways to store the score information for resubmitting it later; however, I feel that the following approach is the easiest for the novice to implement. Feel free to implement your own system if you feel that the provided one does not suit the needs of your app.

There are three steps that need to be completed to handle and recover from a score submitting failure. The first step is to save the score data. Although we do not inform the user of the failure in this example, it is a good idea to notify the user that their score could not be submitted at this time and that you will automatically retry later. Modify the following function in GameCenterManager to match the following code:

```
static func reportScore(score: Int, to leaderboard:
GKLeaderboard, using context: Int, completion: ((Error?) ->
())?) {
    leaderboard.submitScore(score, context: context, player:
    GKLocalPlayer.local) { (error) in
        if error != nil {
        self.storeScoreForLater(
            with: StoredScore(
                score: score,
                leaderboardId: leaderboard.
                baseLeaderboardID,
                context: context,
                playerId: GKLocalPlayer.local.gamePlayerID
            )
        )
    }
}
```

```
        if let completion = completion {
            completion(error)
        }
    }
}
```

We have added a few additional lines of code that will run if an error is detected; if it is, then the NSData from the GKScore is captured and saved. We will later retrieve the GKScore from this NSData. We also call a new function that we have named storeScoreForLater. Let's take a look at that function now; add the following function to the implementation of the GameCenterManager class:

```
private static func storeScoreForLater(with score:
StoredScore) {
    var savedScores: [StoredScore] = []

    if let data = UserDefaults.standard.data(forKey:
    savedScoresKey) {
        savedScores = (try? JSONDecoder().decode([StoredScore].
        self, from: data)) ?? []
    }
    savedScores.append(score)

    UserDefaults.standard.setValue(try? JSONEncoder().
    encode(savedScores), forKey: savedScoresKey)
}
```

This snippet of code will save the NSData that represents our score to the user defaults. You could also write this data to a file or even store it in core data. Never assume the user has only one unsubmitted score; they may have racked up a number of scores across many different leaderboards while playing offline.

We caught a posting failure as well as saved the score to disk to be retried later. The last remaining step is to attempt to resubmit the score to Game Center. This step can be very complex, depending on how intelligent you want the system to be. Most failures of score submissions are related to network access issues but could also be caused by Game Center being down or even a DNS issue.

There is no correct answer as to when to repost a score, but the guideline is that you don't want to hold on to a score that could be submitted. Before we worry about where to tie in the method to resubmit failed scores, let's first implement a method to retry a score posting. Add the following method to your GameCenterManager class:

```
func submitAllSavedScores() {
        let defaults = UserDefaults.standard

        if let savedScoresData = defaults.data(forKey: Self.
        savedScoresKey) {
            defaults.removeObject(forKey: Self.savedScoresKey)

            if let savedScores = try? JSONDecoder().
            decode([SavedScore].self, from: savedScoresData) {
                savedScores.forEach { savedScore in
                    GKLeaderboard.submitScore(savedScore.score,
                    context: 0, player: GKLocalPlayer.local,
                    leaderboardIDs: [savedScore.category]) {
                    [weak self] error in
                        if let error = error {
                            print("An error occurred while
                            submitting a score. Data will be
                            saved to UserDefaults: \(error.
                            localizedDescription)")
                            self?.storeScoreForLater(savedScore)
                        } else {
```

```
                        print("Saved score submitted")
                    }
                }
            }
        }
    }
}
```

The preceding code will loop through all of the saved scores and attempt to resubmit them. We simply log any successes and failures to add back to our array of non-submitted scores for retrying again later.

As mentioned earlier, there are dozens of ways to tie back in resubmitting failed scores. To keep it simple, we add a call to the submitAllSavedScores after we properly authenticate with Game Center. Modify the authenticateLocalUser method of GameCenterManager to match the following:

```
static func authenticateLocalUser(completion:
((UIViewController?, Error?) -> ())?) {
        guard GKLocalPlayer.local.authenticateHandler == nil
        else {
            return
        }

        GKLocalPlayer.local.authenticateHandler = {
        (viewController, error) in
            if error != nil {
                if let completion = completion {
                    completion(nil, error)
                    return
                }
            } else {
```

```
if let completion = completion, let
viewController = viewController {
    completion(viewController, nil)
}

self.submitAllSavedScores()
    }
}
```

Presenting a Leaderboard

Now that we have a leaderboard configured in App Store Connect, and populated a score into that leaderboard, it is time to present the leaderboard to the user. There are two ways of presentation: the first is with Apple's GUI; the second is with a custom GUI. This section will take a look at the implementation using Apple's GUI. In the next section, you will learn how to present a leaderboard with custom graphics by accessing the raw data for the leaderboard directly.

Before we can begin, we need to create a new button that will trigger the leaderboard. We want to do this outside of the game screen because you do not want to drag the user away from a game in progress to view a leaderboard. Begin by adding a new button to the UFOViewController view, as shown in Figure 3-8.

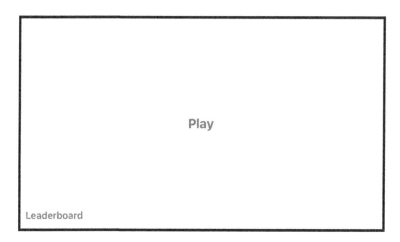

Figure 3-8. *Adding a leaderboard button*

Hook up the button to a new action that matches the one shown next. When leaderboards were first introduced into Game Center, it was required to set up which leaderboard you wanted to launch to. In more recent versions of Game Center, the leaderboards share a combined Leaderboard interface in which the user can navigate to whatever leaderboard they want to view.

```
@IBAction func leaderboardButtonTapped(sender: UIButton) {
    let leaderboardController = GKGameCenterViewController
    (state: .leaderboards)
        leaderboardController.gameCenterDelegate =
        self  present(leaderboardController, animated: true)
}
```

When you run the program and click the newly added Leaderboard button, the result should look similar to the image in Figure 3-9. It is worth noting that while the underlying APIs for GameKit and Game Center aren't updated with great frequency, the UI that Apple uses to represent Game Center changes rapidly and frequently. Not only does the interface change, but some of the navigation has changed in the past as well. For example, in the original versions of leaderboards, the user would be presented directly to the leaderboards for the game they were accessing; in the current implementation, the user is taken to an overview section of leaderboards for the current game.

Figure 3-9. *A leaderboard being presented using Apple's GUI*

The GUI provides a back button to take us to a list of all the leaderboards (see initial view in Figure 3-10) that we have configured for the app. If you omit entering a category when you create the GKLeaderboardViewController instance, you will be presented with whatever leaderboard has been selected as the default leaderboard in App Store Connect.

This is all there is to creating and presenting a leaderboard using Apple's GUI. In the next section, we will look at how to customize a leaderboard to match your own GUI.

Note   Remember that you cannot access any Game Center functionality, including leaderboards, before a local user has authenticated. If you try to do so, you will receive a GKErrorNotAuthenticated error.

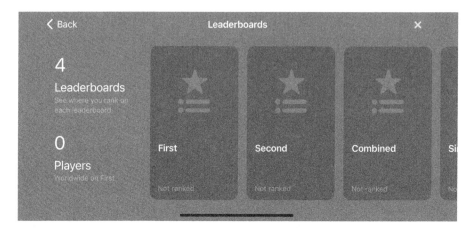

Figure 3-10. *A collection of leaderboards, shown with Apple's GUI*

Tip   You can change the order that leaderboards appear
(see Figure 3-10) by dragging leaderboard entries up and down in
App Store Connect.

Customizing the Leaderboard

As demonstrated in the previous section, presenting a leaderboard to
the user is straightforward. However, what if you want to customize the
appearance of a leaderboard? In this section, you will be walked through
the process of receiving the raw leaderboard information so that you can
present it in your app in whatever fashion suits your needs.

We begin the process of adding a custom leaderboard by adding a
new button and associated action for it to UFOViewController. Add a new
button adjacent to the previous leaderboard button, and create a new
action for it.

In the previous example, Apple provides a view controller for us. When we are working with our own custom leaderboards, we need to create a view controller to handle the presentation. Create a new subclass of UIViewController, and name it UFOLeaderboardViewController. Modify the action of the new custom leaderboard button to present a new instance of UFOLeaderboardViewController, as seen in the following code snippet:

```
@IBAction func customLeaderboardButtonPressed() {
    let leaderboardViewController =
    UFOLeaderboardViewController()
    leaderboardViewController.gcManager = gcManager
    present(leaderboardViewController, animated: true)
}
```

The next step is to set up the storyboard for the new UFOLeaderboard ViewController. We will use the setup as shown in Figure 3-11; however, you may provide whatever kind of customization you want here. Create the outlets and objects, as shown in the figure, and hook up connections for all of them, including the delegate and data source for the table.

Figure 3-11. *Creating the xib for a custom leaderboard*

If you were to run the app at this point and click the Custom Leaderboard button, it should launch a blank table in the correct orientation and allow you to dismiss it to return to the first view.

Now that we got the view controller overhead out of the way, we can begin to focus on the Game Center–specific features. First, set up the table view delegate and data source methods that we will be using. We need to create a new class property to hold the score data for display. Create a new NSArray object and name it scoreArray. Add the following two functions to your implementation:

```
extension UFOLeaderboardViewController: UITableViewDataSource {
    func tableView(_ tableView: UITableView,
    numberOfRowsInSection section: Int) -> Int {
        return scoreArray?.count ?? 0
    }

    static let tableViewCellIdentifier = "Cell"

    func tableView(_ tableView: UITableView, cellForRowAt
    indexPath: IndexPath) -> UITableViewCell {

        var cell = tableView.dequeueReusableCell(wi
        thIdentifier: UFOLeaderboardViewController.
        tableViewCellIdentifier)
        if cell == nil {
            cell = UITableViewCell(style: .subtitle,
            reuseIdentifier: UFOLeaderboardViewController.
            tableViewCellIdentifier)
            cell?.selectionStyle = .none
        }
```

```
    let score = scoreArray?[indexPath.row] as?
    GKLeaderboard.Entry

    let playerName = score?.player.alias

    if playerName == nil {
        cell?.textLabel?.text = "Loading Name..."
    } else {
        cell?.textLabel?.text = playerName
    }

    cell?.detailTextLabel?.text = score?.formattedScore

    return cell!
    }
}
```

The first function returns the number of items in our table view. We deal with only one section in this example, so the number of rows will always equal the number of scores that are in our array. The next function displays the score into the cell. We use UITableViewCellStyleSubtitle in this example, but in most cases, you will want to create a more customized cell. The main label is set to the player alias, and the secondary label is set to the formatted score value. In the previous chapter, it was noted that you should never show a player ID to the user.

Modifying GameCenterManager

Let's take a moment to switch over to our GameCenterManager class.

We create a new function to retrieve scores from the Game Center servers. Add the following method to the GameCenterManager class:

```
static func retrieveScores(from leaderboard: GKLeaderboard,
playerScope: GKLeaderboard.PlayerScope, timeScope:
GKLeaderboard.TimeScope, range: ClosedRange<Int>,
completion: ((GKLeaderboard.Entry?, [GKLeaderboard.Entry]?,
Int, Error?) -> ())?) {
    leaderboard.loadEntries(for: playerScope, timeScope:
    timeScope, range: NSRange(range.clamped(to: 1...100))) {
    (localPlayerEntry, entries, totalPlayerCount, error) in
        if let completion = completion {
            completion(localPlayerEntry, entries,
            totalPlayerCount, error)
        }
    }
}
}
```

We want to keep this call as generic as possible because the ultimate goal of the GameCenterManager class is to be a reusable class that can easily be dropped into any of your future projects.

The preceding method takes all the arguments that are required to create a new GKLeaderboard object. Once we have created the object and set the properties that are required, we can call the method loadScoresWithCompletionHandler on the GKLeaderboard object.

These are all the modifications that are needed in the GameCenterManager class for this section.

Filtering Results on a Custom Leaderboard

Let's shift our focus back to the UFOLeaderboardViewController class again. We will next add an action for our segmented controller. This will allow the user to switch between global scores and friends-only scores. Connect the following method to the valueChanged action of the segmented controller:

```
@IBAction func scopeChanged(_ sender: UISegmentedControl) {
    scores = []

    if let leaderboard = GameCenterManager.leaderboard {
        GameCenterManager.retrieveScores(from: leaderboard,
        playerScope: scopeSegmentedControl.selectedSegmentIndex
        == 0 ? .friendsOnly : .global, timeScope: .allTime,
        range: 1...50) { (localPlayerEntry, entries,
        totalPlayerCount, error) in
            if let error = error {
                print("An error occurred: \(error.
                localizedDescription)")
            } else {
                self.scores = entries ?? []
            }

            self.tableView.reloadData()
        }
    }
}
```

This method calls the GameCenterManager method to retrieve our score list. The segmented control has two values: one for friends and one for everyone (global). You could easily modify the preceding code to retrieve different time scopes as well, but in this example, we request only the all-time scope. An important step here that can be easy to overlook is setting the array to an empty array and reloading the table. Doing so will remove the scores that are in the table when the segmented controller value is changed.

The retrieve scores call is fairly straightforward. We use the category we set in App Store Connect for the leaderboard we wish to retrieve and set our time and player scope. The last argument on the method is a range. In the previous example, we return scores from 1st place to 50th place.

Note   Score ranges always start at an index of 1. You could modify the preceding example with a new range of NSMakeRange(50,50); this will retrieve scores from 50th place to 100th place. Make sure you don't request too many scores at a time, as the time it takes to retrieve the score data is related to how many scores you are attempting to retrieve.

Displaying the Custom Leaderboard

If you were to run this project now, you would notice the table is always blank. This is caused by an omission. To rectify this, modify the existing IBAction method to set the property for gameCenterDelegate to the instance that exists in the UFOViewController. Your code should look like the following example:

```
@IBAction func leaderboardButtonTapped(sender: UIButton) {
    let leaderboardController = GKGameCenterViewController(state: .leaderboards)
    leaderboardController.gameCenterDelegate = self
    present(leaderboardController, animated: true)
}
```

If you were to now run the app again, you would see output similar to that shown in Figure 3-12. The number of scores, the score values, and the player alias will be different, but you should be able to see at least one score listed.

Figure 3-12. *An initial view of our custom leaderboard*

Important   It cannot be guaranteed that you will not be returned cached data for a leaderboard request. You should assume that the data you are retrieving is cached and might not be the most up-to-date.

Local Player Score

There are oftentimes that you will want to know the local players' score on a given leaderboard. Maybe you want to display their scores at the top of your leaderboard, or perhaps you want to fetch a leaderboard that shows other player scores that are close to your local player's score. You can even want to post an action in the game when the user has beaten their own previous high score.

Apple has provided an easy technique for determining the local players' score. Once you have a reference to the leaderboard you are interested in finding a local score for, all that needs to be done is query the property for localPlayerScore.

```
print(leaderboard.localPlayerScore)
```

75

A Better Approach

In the section "Posting a Score," earlier in this chapter, we discovered how to post new scores to Game Center. Our methodology, while simple, was not the best approach from a user-interaction standpoint. It is now time to refactor the posting new score code to improve usability. This approach is more complex but delivers better performance and has less of an impact on the user.

The first thing we need to do is move our scoreReported function from UFOGameViewController to UFOViewController. We also want to modify the exit action in the UFOViewController to report the score back to Game Center.

This allows us to exit the game without waiting for a network callback from the Game Center delegate.

Game Center Groups

A more recent addition to Game Center functionality allowed for Game Center Groups, or more succulently sharing a leaderboard or achievement across multiple different apps. Some caveats exist and need to be considered before moving to a Game Center Group; most notably all the apps must exist under the state App Store Connect account; there is no way to set up a Game Center Group between apps under different accounts.

In order to set up a new Game Center Group, you must first launch the Game Center area of the App Store Connect portal for the first app you want to add to the group. There is a small section to set up a new group; see Figure 3-13.

Important   If your app has an existing leaderboard, their leaderboard IDs will be listed with a "grp." prefix. You can keep the ID the same or create a new one when setting them up.

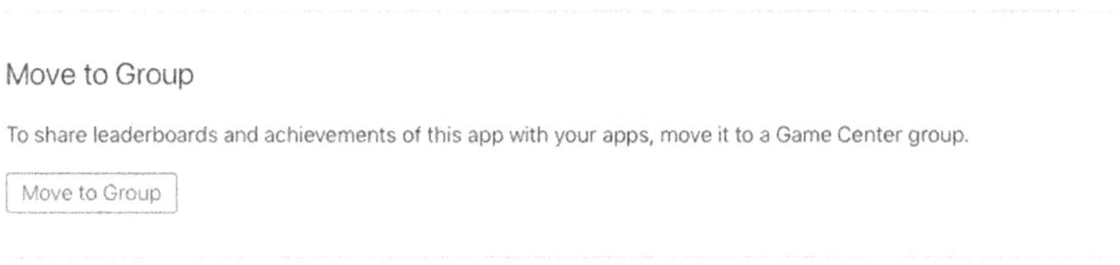

Move to Group

To share leaderboards and achievements of this app with your apps, move it to a Game Center group.

Move to Group

Figure 3-13. *Setting up a Game Center Group*

You may selectively pick which leaderboards and achievements will be part of each group, and the process is reversable to the point where you may delete the entire group if you later desire. If your app already has existing leaderboards (or achievements), you must decide whether to merge those items with the group items. You may of course also create new group-specific leaderboards and achievements.

All functionality of Game Center Groups is controlled via the App Store Connect portal, and it will guide you through merging and controlling leaderboards and achievements just as you would do with a non-group leaderboard or achievement.

Accessing the leaderboards from within your app is exactly the same whether it is a group or not; you will just need the app to be part of the respected group and reference the provided (or created) leaderboard ID.

Summary

This chapter introduced leaderboards in Game Center. We covered the benefits of using a leaderboard, as well as the two available types. We learned how to post a score and recover for any errors that occurred during posting. We also looked at the requirements of getting leaderboards up and running in your app, using either Apple's provided GUI or a custom one.

Throughout the chapter, we continued to build our GameCenterManager class, adding the required methods to post scores, retrieve scores both local and global, and display custom and built-in leaderboards. You should now feel confident in adding a leaderboard to any existing or new iOS app. In the next chapter, we will explore all that Game Center achievements offer.

CHAPTER 4

Achievements

The relatively new gaming concept, achievements, came along much later than leaderboards and has gained a dramatic rise in popularity with the release of Microsoft's Xbox 360 and newer devices. Achievements offer a higher level of detail overlooked in more basic leaderboards. While leaderboards show who currently possesses the leading scores, achievements demonstrate a player's skills and strengths by rewarding the player for completing more specific tasks, events, or levels. When the achievements start to serve in-game purposes, they become more of a power-up over other players. The ability to view the achievements by others gives players a type of "bragging rights." As you are of no doubt aware, bragging rights in a game can extend gameplay for a variety of users trying to reach 100% completeness, to maintain their lead over their peers, or to knock a peer from the top.

As social network–enabled gaming spreads and becomes prevalent, the achievement system feature has skyrocketed into even more popularity. Social games are filled with a niche player base determined to complete 100% of the game.

Foursquare was one of the first to bring achievements out of the gaming world and into the social app universe. Foursquare calls its achievements "stickers" (see Figure 4-1), but the basic concept is the same. Players receive a reward for completing a task, but the number of badges does not affect gameplay or, in this case, the ability for the user to use the app in any direct manner.

© Kyle Richter and Beau G. Bolle 2022
K. Richter and B. G. Bolle, *Beginning iOS Game Center and GameKit*,
https://doi.org/10.1007/978-1-4842-7756-0_4

Figure 4-1. *Foursquare for iPhone showing achievements, renamed Stickers in later versions*

Game Center has made adding an achievement system to your iOS, Mac, or Apple TV app simple. In this chapter, we will learn how to add achievements to our demo game, UFOs. You will learn everything needed to fully integrate an achievement system into your app quickly and easily. Notably, you will learn how to:

- Create new achievements

- Display achievement progress

- Add achievement hooks into your app

- Progress and reset achievements
- Customize the appearance of achievements

Why Achievements?

If it is not already apparent what achievements can add to your social app or game, let's take a moment to review some of the many benefits:

- Achievements give your users an extra sense of accomplishment and reward.

- Achievements bring users back into your app more often. Users are more likely to return to your app to complete more achievements, making completing the game a more rewarding and fun process.

- Achievements add an easy way for users to share experiences with other users.

- Achievements in Game Center provide a polished look and feel to the shipping product.

- Achievements give users a greater sense of progression as they make their way through your app or game.

- Achievements provide an alternative way to play the game. If users do not enjoy the campaign, they can enjoy a sense of accomplishment through your achievement system.

- Achievements attribute game brand awareness. As users share their accomplishments on Twitter, Facebook, and other social platforms, name recognition increases and in hand sales.

An Overview of Achievements in Game Center

Achievements, also known as badges in certain circles, function slightly differently in Game Center than on other platforms. As with leaderboards, achievements first need to be configured in App Store Connect on a per-app basis. You will be creating new instances of a GKAchievement object to report progress (more on this object later). Unlike leaderboard entries, which are created when a score is reached and submitted, achievements can report incremental or partial progress.

Another notable change from working with leaderboards (see Chapter 3 for more on leaderboards) is that you will use two different types of objects to submit and retrieve achievements. GKAchievement is used to submit new achievements or update progress on achievements, and GKAchievementDescription is used to display achievement data to the user. This is contrary to what we saw when working with leaderboards, in which GKScore objects were used to submit data as well as retrieve it.

As with leaderboards, achievement progress can be shown using either Apple's included graphical user interface (GUI) or a customized one that better matches the look and feel of your app. The advantages and disadvantages of each system are the same as with leaderboards. Those advantages and disadvantages follow for your convenience, with minor achievement-specific information added where appropriate.

Benefits of Using Apple's Achievement GUI vs. a Custom GUI

The following are some of the benefits that you will gain by using Apple's included GUI for working with achievements:

- The look and feel of your achievements are created by some of the best designers in the world.

- The GUI is very simple and easy to implement, making it straightforward to present the achievement progress to your users.

- Users appreciate a familiar interface with which they already know how to interact.

- Your app is more future-proof than it otherwise would be if you implemented your own system. Every revision of Game Center user interfaces is automatically taken advantage of by your app.

The following are a few of the benefits of using your own GUI when working with achievements on iOS devices:

- Your achievement progress can match the custom design of your app.

- You have more freedom over the returned data and can filter using additional criteria.

- You can implement your own custom caching behavior.

- You can use custom images for incomplete or in-progress achievements.

As you can see, as always, there are advantages and disadvantages of each system, and there is no right answer in which one you should be using. By the end of this chapter, you will have a better understanding of the options and be better equipped to decide which approach is the best fit for your app.

As mentioned in the beginning of this section, you will need to begin with achievements in the same manner as we did for leaderboards, in App Store Connect.

Configuring Achievements in App Store Connect

As we saw with leaderboards, you cannot begin working with achievements without first setting up at least one new achievement in App Store Connect. Log in to App Store Connect (`http://appstoreconnect.apple.com`) using your Apple connect username and password, and select the app that we have already been working with from the previous chapters (see Chapter 2 for more information). Once you have selected your app from the control panel, return to the Manage Features and then Game Center area that was introduced earlier in this book.

The Game Center portal for your app will have a section labeled "Achievements." You will find a "+" button in the upper left area of the achievement area. This button will allow you to set up a new achievement as seen in Figure 4-2.

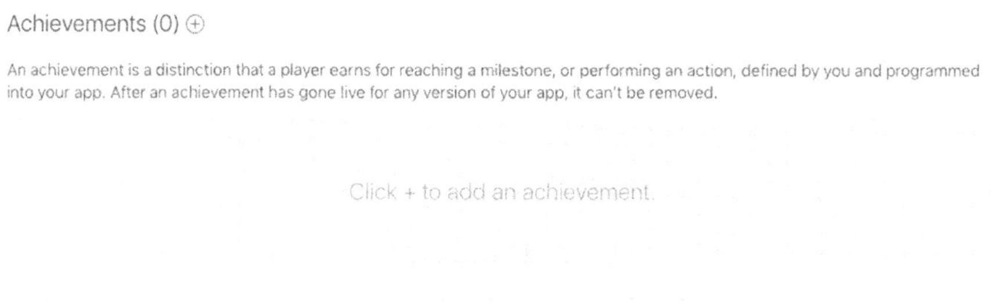

Achievements (0) ⊕

An achievement is a distinction that a player earns for reaching a milestone, or performing an action, defined by you and programmed into your app. After an achievement has gone live for any version of your app, it can't be removed.

Click + to add an achievement.

Figure 4-2. *Adding a new achievement through the App Store Connect portal*

You might notice that there are a lot of similarities between this portal page and the leaderboard portal page. I break down the attributes in Table 4-1.

Table 4-1. *Achievement Attributes in iTunes Connect*

Attribute	Description
Achievement reference name	A string that is not used outside of iTunes Connect; this string is used to easily locate and reference this achievement within App Store Connect.
Achievement ID	This is the identifier that you will refer to in your code. As with leaderboard categories, Apple recommends that you use a reverse DNS system such as com.company.appname.achievementname.
Hidden	If an achievement is hidden, the user will not see it in the achievement list until they have either completed it or increased the progress.
Point value	Achievements can be assigned points. Your app is allocated 1,000 points. Each completed achievement progresses the user toward that total. Once the user has reached 1,000 points, they have unlocked all achievements. You should assign more points to achievements that are more difficult to complete. This provides the user with a better sense of how valuable the achievement is. Point values are optional and can be ignored if you do not want to use them within your app.

Tip   You aren't required to have your achievements add up to 1,000 total points, but you cannot exceed 1,000 points. Be careful of figuring in any future achievements you might want to add. Once an achievement has gone live, it cannot be removed from App Store Connect; however, it can be removed and hidden from your game.

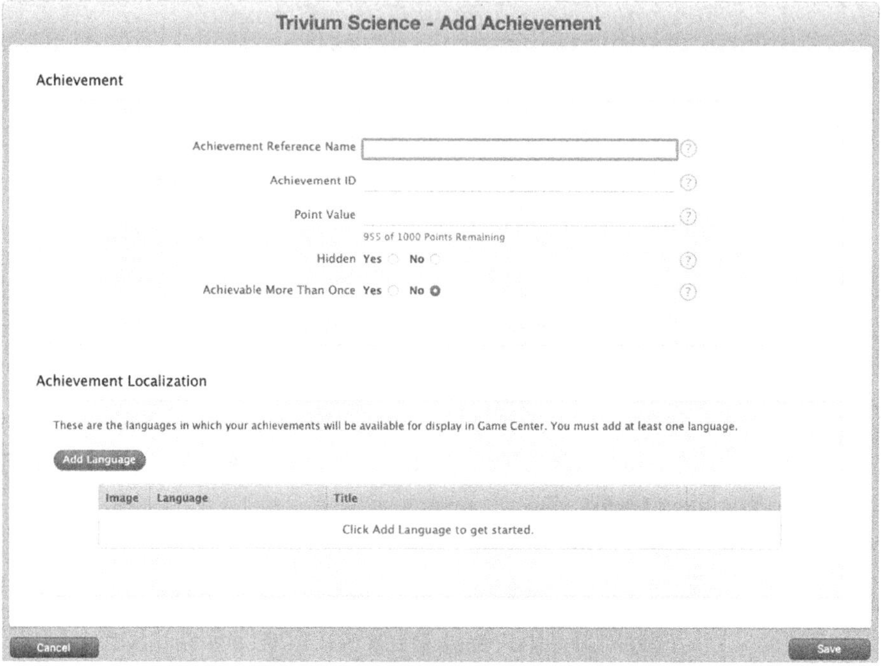

Figure 4-3. *The configuration view for new achievements in App Store Connect*

It is now time to make a new achievement. We will create an achievement that will be reached when the user abducts 25 cows. We will use "Abduct 25" for the achievement name so it will be easy to find when we have dozens of achievements. For our achievement ID, we will use "com.dragonforged.ufo.abduct25." Feel free to use whatever ID you want here, but make sure to substitute it for com.dragonforged.ufo.abduct25 in the upcoming examples. We will make this an unhidden achievement and assign it a point value of 10.

Important   No achievement can have more than 100 points awarded for completing it.

For an achievement to be valid, you must configure at least one language. As you can see in Figure 4-4, the localization area of achievements is much different than that encountered when creating leaderboards in the previous chapter. Refer to Table 4-2 for information on each attribute.

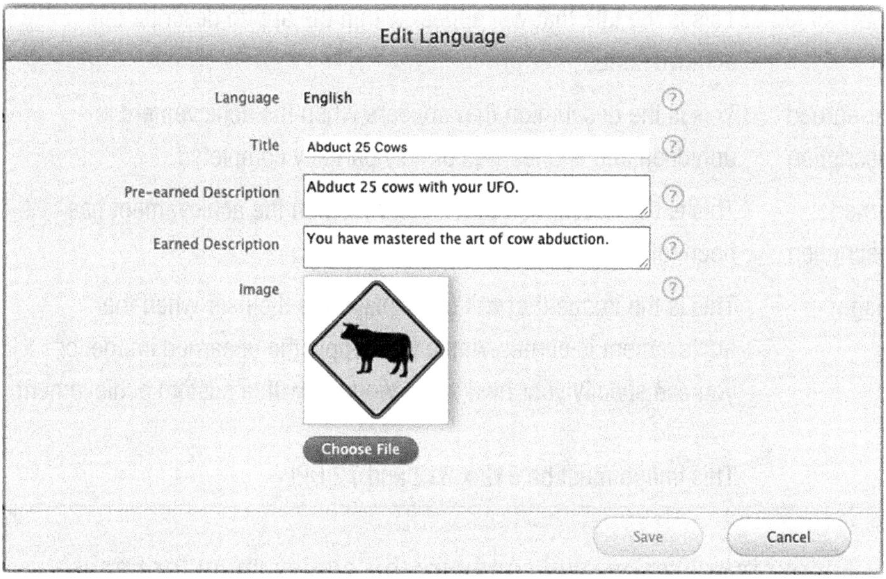

Figure 4-4. *Localizing an achievement in iTunes Connect*

Note   Each game owns its achievement descriptions; you may not share achievement descriptions between multiple games.

Table 4-2. *Localized Achievement Attributes in iTunes Connect*

Attribute	Description
Language	Select the language in which this achievement will appear. You must set up a language for each localization that you will support in your shipping product.
Title	This is the title that will appear within the app to describe this achievement.
Pre-earned description	This is the description that appears when the achievement is unhidden and is unearned or only partially completed.
Earned description	This is the description that is shown when the achievement has been fully unlocked and completed.
Image	This is the image that will be displayed to the user when the achievement is earned. Apple will supply the unearned image, or you can specify your own when working with a custom achievement GUI. This image must be 512 x 512 and 72 DPI.

For our purposes, we will configure this achievement for English. I will use "Abduct 25 Cows" as the title, but you may use any title that you prefer. For the pre-earned description, I chose "Abduct 25 cows with your UFO." For the earned description, I used "You have mastered the art of cow abduction." I will also use a cow crossing road sign as the image. When you are done, you should have a fully set up achievement, which should look similar to the view shown in Figure 4-5.

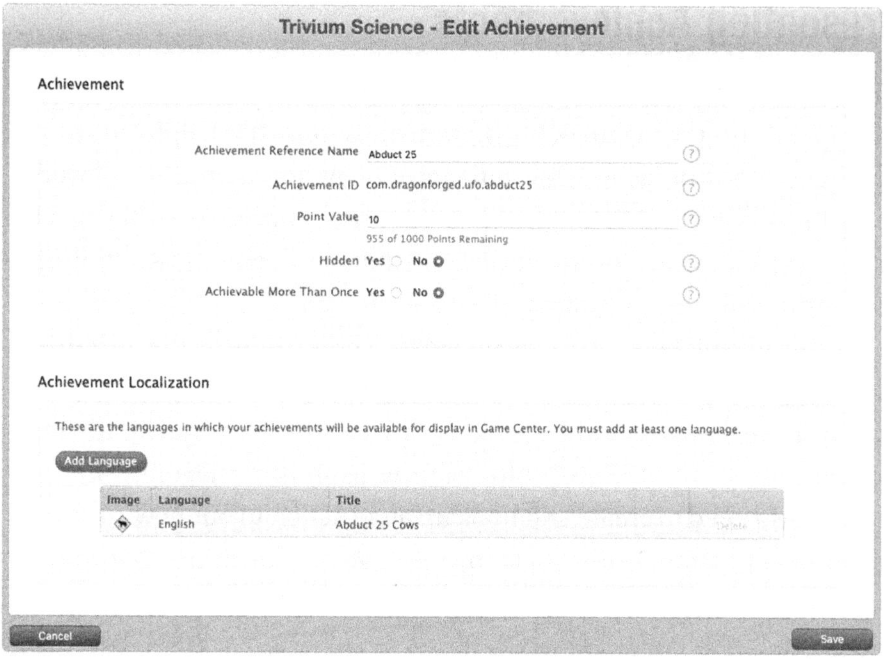

Trivium Science - Edit Achievement

Achievement

Achievement Reference Name Abduct 25

Achievement ID com.dragonforged.ufo.abduct25

Point Value 10
955 of 1000 Points Remaining

Hidden Yes ○ No ◉

Achievable More Than Once Yes ○ No ◉

Achievement Localization

These are the languages in which your achievements will be available for display in Game Center. You must add at least one language.

Add Language

Image	Language	Title
🐄	English	Abduct 25 Cows

Cancel   Save

Figure 4-5. *A new achievement, as shown in iTunes Connect*

We will want to work with a couple of different achievement setups for our game. Go ahead and create another new achievement for abducting a single cow; this will be our nonprogressive achievement. Then, make a third achievement for five-minute playtime and set it to hidden. This last achievement will let us work with timers, progressive achievements, and hidden achievements. You may select any point values, descriptions, titles, and images you want for these achievements, but make sure you remember the achievement IDs.

You should now have three achievements configured in App Store Connect for our game.

We can now get back into Xcode and begin working with these achievements.

Presenting Achievements

Unlike leaderboards, there will be plenty to preview GUI-wise before we populate user data into our achievement system. It is helpful to see the effects that modifying achievements have on how they are displayed through the default GUI. In the remainder of this chapter, we will begin by presenting Apple's achievement GUI and then move on to submitting user data. We will also cover custom GUI achievements.

Before we can begin, we need to create a new UIbutton that will trigger the achievement view. We most likely want to do this outside of the game screen, as we did with our two leaderboard buttons. We begin by adding a new button to the UFOViewController view, as shown in Figure 4-6.

You also need to create and hook up an IBAction to our new achievement button. Insert the following code into the action that you hooked up to the achievement button:

```
@IBAction func achievementButtonPressed() {
    var achievementViewController: GKGameCenterViewController?
    = nil
    if let state = GKGameCenterViewControllerState(
    rawValue: 1) {
        achievementViewController = GKGameCenterView
        Controller(state: state)
    }
    achievementViewController?.gameCenterDelegate = self
    if let achievementViewController =
    achievementViewController {
        present(achievementViewController, animated: true)
    }
}
```

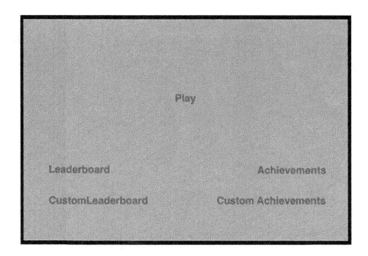

Figure 4-6. *Adding a new button to trigger our achievement view*

If you were to run the App and tap on the achievement button, you would now see a view similar to the one shown in Figure 4-7. The achievements shown are using Apple's unearned image. Apple recommends that you always use its unearned image, but when working with a custom achievement GUI, you can override this image and return your own.

Next, recall that we set up three achievements, one of them hidden. As you can see in Figure 4-7, the provided view shows us only two achievements. Because we have not submitted any kind of progress to the third achievement, its details are hidden from the user. However, you can see that the top information line reflects that there is a hidden achievement (0 of 3 achievements). Also notice that the achievements are using the localized unearned description that was set in iTunes Connect.

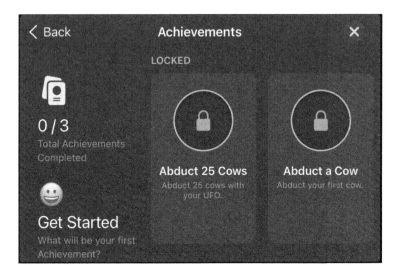

Figure 4-7. *Our achievements, as shown with Apple's default GUI*

These are the only necessary steps to show the user his or her achievement progress through Apple's built-in GUI. In the next section, we will look at how to update and progress these achievements. Later in this chapter, you will learn how to present achievement using a custom GUI.

Note   A user can always see his or her achievement progress in Game Center, but it is recommended allowing your user a way to view their progress from within your app as well.

Modifying Achievement Progress

Unlike a leaderboard entry, achievements can be constantly modified and progressed through user interaction. As with the other Game Center functionality we have been working with, we will create a new method in our GameCenterManager class to handle interacting with achievements. Once the following method has been added, we will review the method to understand exactly how it functions.

Tip   Remember that all this source code is made available to you online. When dealing with large functions, it might be easier to copy it from the source code downloaded from apress.com.

```swift
func submitAchievement(_ identifier: String,
percentComplete: Double) {
    if GKLocalPlayer.local.isAuthenticated == false {
        return
    }
    guard earnedAchievementCache != nil else {
        populateAchievementCache() {
            self.submitAchievement(identifier,
            percentComplete: percentComplete)
        }
        return
    }

    if let achievement = achievement(forIdentifier:
    identifier) {
        let storedProgress = achievement.percentComplete

        guard percentComplete > storedProgress else {
            return
        }

        achievement.percentComplete = percentComplete

        GKAchievement.report([achievement],
        withCompletionHandler: { [weak self] error in
```

```swift
    if let error = error {
        print("An error occurred while
         reporting an achievement. Data will
         be saved to UserDefaults: \(error.
         localizedDescription)")
        self?.storeAchievementToSubmitLater(
        achievement)
    }

    if percentComplete >= 100 {
        GKAchievementDescription.loadAchievementDes
        criptions(completionHandler: { [weak self]
        achievementDescriptions, error in
            if let error = error {
                print("An error occurred while
                loading achievement descriptions:
                \(error.localizedDescription)")
            }
            achievementDescriptions?.forEach{
            achievementDescription in
                if achievement.identifier ==
                achievementDescription.identifier {
                    self?.gameDelegate?.achievement
                    Earned(achievementDescription)
                }
            }
        })
    }

    DispatchQueue.main.async { [weak self] in
        self?.gameDelegate?.achievementSubmitted(
        achievement, error: error)
    }
```

```
        })
    }

  }

}
```

Now look at the submitAchievement:percentComplete: function we added. There are two primary if/else blocks. The first one is executed if earnedAchievementCache is nil, which it will always be the first time this code is executed. Let's take a look at that block of code now.

```
GKAchievement.loadAchievements(completionHandler: {
achievements, error in
            if error == nil {
                var tempCache: [String: GKAchievement] = [:]
                for achievement in achievements ?? [] {
                    tempCache[achievement.identifier] =
                    achievement
                }
                self.earnedAchievementCache = tempCache as?
                NSMutableDictionary
                self.submitAchievement(identifier,
                percentComplete: percentComplete)
            } else {
                DispatchQueue.main.async {
                    self.delegate?.
                    achievementSubmitted?(nil, error:
                    error)
                }
            }
        })
```

Important   The array that is returned by loadAchievements
WithCompletionHandler will not show any achievements that you
have not yet submitted a percentageCompleted for.

The primary function of this code snippet is to load a list
of achievements into the earnedAchievementCache. We call
loadAchievementsWithCompletionHandler on GKAchievement. This
call returns an array of all the achievements that were set up in App Store
Connect. We then store the GKAchievement object into the dictionary with
the identifier as the key. At this point, the code calls submitAchievement
:percentComplete again. This time, earnedAchievementCache is not nil
and the second set of code is executed. If we encounter an error during this
process, we use our standard delegate callback to send the error back to
our delegate.

You will need to add new functions to GameCenterManager to handle
this delegate callback; this is a good time to do that. Add the following
optional protocol to the header file:

```
func achievementSubmitted(_ achievement: GKAchievement?,
error: Error?)
```

Now let's take a look at the second section of code. The following code,
when successfully executed, submits the achievement to the Game Center
servers:

```
var achievement = earnedAchievementCache?[identifier ?? ""] as?
GKAchievement
            if achievement != nil {
                if ((achievement?.percentComplete ?? 0.0) >=
                100.0) || ((achievement?.percentComplete ??
                0.0) >= percentComplete) {
```

```swift
            achievement = nil
        }
        achievement?.percentComplete = percentComplete
    } else {
        achievement = GKAchievement(identifier:
        identifier ?? "")
        achievement?.percentComplete = percentComplete
        earnedAchievementCache?.setValue(achievement,
        forKey: achievement?.identifier ?? "")
    }

    if let achievement = achievement {
        GKAchievement.report([achievement],
        withCompletionHandler: { error in
            if error != nil {
                self.storeAchievement(toSubmitLater:
                achievement)
            }

            if percentComplete >= 100 {
                GKAchievement.loadAchievements(completion
                Handler: { achievements, error in
                    for achievementDescription in
                    achievements ?? [] {
                        if achievement.
                        identifier == self.
                        from(achievementDescription).
                        identifier {
                            self.delegate?.achievement
                            Earned?(self.from(
                            achievementDescription))
                        }
```

```
                }
            })
        }
        DispatchQueue.main.async {
            self.delegate?.achievementSubmitted?(
            achievement, error: error)
        }
    })
}
```

The first line of code retrieves a GKAchievement object from our earnedAchievementCache, based on the identifier string that is passed into this function. If the achievement is completed or the reported progress is equal to what we have on the Game Center server, we set the achievement to nil. This prevents us from tying up networking time by submitting progress on something that will be ignored. We also set the property for percentComplete on the GKAchievement object to the double that was passed into this method.

In the event that the achievement doesn't exist in the cache, we create a new instance of it. In this event, we also want to add it to our local achievement cache.

The final step, after doing a nil check, is to submit the achievement. We call reportAchievementWithCompletionHandler on the achievement object. We then pass the results back to our delegate using our existing protocol.

Note   All achievements have a percentageComplete regardless of whether they allow a percentage to be completed at a time. If your achievement can only be completely earned or unearned, then you will want to pass 100 for earned.

The last thing that we need to do in this section is implement our protocol method in UFOGameViewController. Add the following method to the implementation of that file; all we will worry about right now is printing the error and success information to the console.

```swift
func achievementSubmitted(_ achievement: GKAchievement?, error:
Error?) {
    if let error = error {
        print("There was an error in reporting the
        achievement: \(error.localizedDescription)")
    } else {
        print("achievement submitted")
    }
}
```

Resetting Achievements

There are circumstances when you might want to reset user achievements. Besides being extremely helpful in debugging, you might find it useful to provide users with an option to reset. You might want to add a prestige mode or give the users a chance to start your game over from the beginning.

```swift
func resetAchievements()
{
    GKAchievement.resetAchievementsWithCompletionHandler()
    {(error) in
        self.lastError = error
    }
}
```

Important   Don't forget to remove the cached information you have stored on the achievements, or you will not be able to progress the reset achievements until the app is restarted.

Adding Achievement Hooks

The biggest challenge in implementing achievements into your app is adding the hooks to activate and progress those achievements into your normal routines. In my personal experience, I have found that adding these hooks when the program is almost finished is easier than trying to add them in as you go. In this section, I will provide a number of examples of how to tie in achievements; your own app may differ significantly, but you should be able to easily adapt the examples to suit your needs.

To make achievements easier to retrieve progress details, we first add a few convenience functions to our GameCenterManager class. This is the first method we will use to populate the local achievement cache.

```swift
func populateAchievementCache(_ completion: (() -> Void)? =
nil) {
        guard earnedAchievementCache == nil else {
            completion?()
            return
        }

        GKAchievement.loadAchievements { [weak self]
        achievements, error in
            if let error = error {
                print("An error occurred while loading
                achievements: \(error.localizedDescription)")
            } else {
```

```
        if let achievements = achievements {
            self?.earnedAchievementCache =
            achievements.reduce(into: [:], { result,
            achievement in
                result[achievement.identifier] =
                achievement
            })
        } else {
            self?.earnedAchievementCache = [:]
        }
        completion?()
    }
  }
}
```

The preceding function is very similar to the cache population code in the submit achievement progress method previewed in the previous section. We will need to populate the local cache in order to work with the other two convenience functions. We will want to call the populateAchievementCache as soon as we can after authenticating. I have added a call to it from the local player did authenticate function in GameCenterManager. Add the following function as well:

```
func percentageCompleteOfAchievement(withIdentifier identifier:
String?) -> Double {
    if GKLocalPlayer.local.isAuthenticated == false {
        return -1
    }

    if earnedAchievementCache == nil {
        print("Unable to determine achievement progress,
        local cache is empty")
    } else {
```

```
            let achievement = earnedAchievementCache?[
            identifier ?? ""]

            if let achievement = achievement {
                return achievement.percentComplete
            } else {
                return 0
            }
        }

    return -1
}
```

The preceding function returns a double for the percentage complete for the achievement with the identifier passed to it. If it cannot find a copy of the achievement in the local cache, we can assume the percentage complete is 0. The next function uses the preceding function to return either YES or NO on whether an achievement has been completed.

```
func achievement(withIdentifierIsComplete identifier: String?)
-> Bool {
    if percentageCompleteOfAchievement(withIdentifier:
    identifier) >= 100 {
        return true
    } else {
        return false
    }
  }
}
```

Note   Do not forget to call populateAchievementCache as soon as possible after authentication. Otherwise, these convenience methods will not return correct information.

Now that we have some helper functions in place, we can begin to hook up the achievement hooks for UFOs. We have three different achievements we need to tie in. The first two both have to do with the number of cows that we have abducted, so let's start there. Modify the finishAbducting function of UFOGameViewController to match the following:

```swift
func finishAbducting() {
    if currentAbductee == nil || !tractorBeamOn {
        return
    }

    cowArray = cowArray?.filter({ ($0) as AnyObject !==
    (currentAbductee) as AnyObject })

    tractorBeamImageView?.removeFromSuperview()

    tractorBeamOn = false

    score += 1
    scoreLabel.text = String(format: "SCORE %05.0f", score)

    if gameIsMultiplayer {
        gcManager?.sendStringToAllPeers("$score:\(score)",
        reliable: true)
    }

    currentAbductee?.layer.removeAllAnimations()
    currentAbductee?.removeFromSuperview()

    currentAbductee = nil

    if isHost {
        spawnCow()
    }
```

```
    if (gcManager?.achievement(withIdentifierIsComplete:
    "com.dragonforged.ufo.aduct1") == false) {
        gcManager?.submitAchievement("com.dragonforged.ufo.
        aduct1", percentComplete: 100)
    }

    if (gcManager?.achievement(withIdentifierIsComplete:
    "com.dragonforged.ufo.abduct25") == false) {
        var percentComplete = gcManager?.percentageComplet
        eOfAchievement(withIdentifier: "com.dragonforged.
        ufo.abduct25") ?? 0.0
        percentComplete += 4
        gcManager?.submitAchievement("com.dragonforged.ufo.
        abduct25", percentComplete: percentComplete)
    }
}
```

We are concerned with only the last few lines of this
method at this time. First, we call our convenience function
achievementWithIdentifierIsComplete on our identifier string for a
single abduction. Because this is an earned or unearned achievement,
we don't need to worry about current percentage complete. To mark the
achievement as complete, we set its percentage complete to 100.

Note   Don't forget to change the identifier string from the example
to the one that you used in App Store Connect for a single abduction
if different.

The next achievement is hooked up in a similar fashion; the only
difference is that we use incremental progress. Look at the newly added
following code snippet onto the end of the finishAbducting function:

```
if (gcManager?.achievement(withIdentifierIsComplete: "com.
dragonforged.ufo.abduct25") == false) {
            var percentComplete = gcManager?.percentageComplete
            OfAchievement(withIdentifier: "com.dragonforged.
            ufo.abduct25") ?? 0.0
            percentComplete += 4
            gcManager?.submitAchievement("com.dragonforged.ufo.
            abduct25", percentComplete: percentComplete)
    }
```

In the preceding code snippet, we use the same methodology that we did for submitting a complete achievement, but with one main difference. We first need to determine the current progress on the achievement. We then add 4 to it, since 4% of 25 is 1. To increment by 1 abduction out of 25, we need to add 4% each time a new cow is abducted.

Tip   Do not forget about the resetAchievement method that we added to GameCenterManager. It is very useful in debugging the submit code. It is helpful to keep a call to this in the didAuthenticate section to always put the app back to a clean state during debugging.

Go ahead and run the game and abduct a few cows. When you are done, you will notice that the achievement screen now shows progress similar to that shown in Figure 4-8. If you abducted at least one cow, you should have a complete achievement. If you abducted less than 25 cows, you should have one progressed achievement. Notice that the user is not informed when he or she completes an achievement; we will discuss a method of notification in the later section, "Achievement Completion Feedback."

Figure 4-8. *Progressing achievements*

The last hook we add for this project handles the player for the five-minute achievement. Your first instinct is probably to keep track of time played and submit it as progress when your user exits the game. This might not be the best approach. We want to inform the user when they complete an achievement. You don't want them to have to wait until they finish a game to see which achievements they have earned. There are many approaches to this problem. For this example, we will fire an NSTimer every three seconds (which is 1% of five minutes) and update the achievements progress. Add the following to UFOGameViewController:

```swift
func tickThreeSeconds() {
    if gcManager?.achievement(withIdentifierIsComplete:
    "com.dragonforged.ufo.play5") == true {
        return
    } else {
        var percentComplete = gcManager?.percentageComplet
        eOfAchievement(withIdentifier: "com.dragonforged.
        ufo.play5") ?? 0.0
```

```
        percentComplete += 1
        gcManager?.submitAchievement("com.dragonforged.ufo.
        play5", percentComplete: percentComplete)
    }
}
```

Same as modifying the viewDidAppear and ViewWillDisappear functions to match the following, we will start a three-second timer. Every time the timer fires, we call tickThreeSeconds. This gives us our current progress of the achievement, to which we add 1%, and then submit it back to the server. In the event that the achievement is already complete, we simply return.

```
override func viewDidAppear(_ animated: Bool) {
    super.viewDidAppear(animated)

    timer = Timer.scheduledTimer(
        timeInterval: 3.0,
        target: self,
        selector: #selector(tickThreeSeconds),
        userInfo: nil,
        repeats: true)
}

override func viewWillDisappear(_ animated: Bool) {
    super.viewWillDisappear(animated)

    timer?.invalidate()
    timer = nil
}
```

Achievement Completion Feedback

It is important to let users know when they have completed an achievement. However, you don't want to just present a UIAlertView, as that would be very distracting, considering most achievements are going to be completed in the middle of an action, such as completing 20 laps in a racing game. You wouldn't want to take the user away from any interaction, so we will need a better system. I have always been a fan of the small view that slides in from the bottom or top to inform the user of the accomplishment—very similar to the fashion in which you get feedback from logging in to Game Center.

The first thing we need to do in order to implement a feedback system is add a new protocol function to GameCenterManager. We will use this to inform the delegate that an achievement has been completed for the first time. Add the following function to the project as an optional protocol:

```
func achievementEarned(_ achievement: GKAchievementDescription?)
```

In addition, we need to modify our existing submitAchievem ent:percentComplete: method. Take a look at the last if statement block of that function. We want to modify it as follows but add an if statement to determine whether we have a percentageComplete over 100, which will call our new protocol. Also notice that we are using GKAchievementDescription instead of GKAchievement. We will discuss this further in the next section, "Custom Achievement GUI."

```
if percentComplete >= 100 {
                GKAchievementDescription.loadAchievementDes
                criptions(completionHandler: { [weak self]
                achievementDescriptions, error in
                    if let error = error {
```

```
            print("An error occurred while
            loading achievement descriptions: \
            (error.localizedDescription)")
        }
        achievementDescriptions?.forEach{
        achievementDescription in
            if achievement.identifier ==
            achievementDescription.identifier {
                self?.delegate?.achievementEarn
                ed(achievementDescription)
            }
        }
    })
}
```

This completes the modifications that we need to make to the GameCenterManager class. Now we need to hook up the visual feedback for the user. Move back into UFOGameViewController.swift, and add our new function achievementEarned. You could add any type of feedback here including a standard UIAlertView, but we will be exploring something a little more user friendly in this section.

We need to create some new IBOutlets as part of our UFOGameViewController. Make a new view. Then, set the background of the view to black with 70% opacity. We also create a new label, place it in the center of this view, and set the text alignment to the center. Your view should look similar to that shown in Figure 4-9.

Figure 4-9. *Achievement earned view and label*

First a new frame is created for the completion view, and it is then added as a subview to the game view.

```
func achievementEarned(_ achievement:
GKAchievementDescription?) {
        achievementCompletionView.frame = CGRect(x: 0, y: 320,
        width: 480, height: 25)
        view.addSubview(achievementCompletionView)
        achievementcompletionLabel.text = achievement?.
        achievedDescription

        UIView.animate(
            withDuration: 0.5,
            animations: {
                self.achievementCompletionView.frame =
                CGRect(x: 0, y: 295, width: 480, height: 25)
            },
            completion: achievementEarnedAnimationDone
        )
    }
```

Both of these functions are fairly straightforward. When we get a delegate callback from completing the achievement, we add our achievementCompletionView to our game view. Then, we animate it onto the bottom of the view. After a five-second delay, we animate it back off the view. You also have access to the images used in GKAchievementDescription. We will look more into these properties in the next section.

Tip   You might need to reset your achievements to see any completion progress. You may find that it is helpful to create a new button that resets achievements for use during testing.

If you run the app now and abduct a single cow (assuming you haven't yet accomplished that achievement), you should see output very similar to that shown in Figure 4-10.

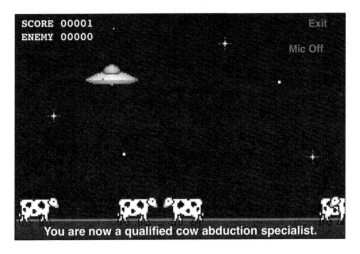

Figure 4-10. *Achievement notification banner visible after completing a new achievement for the first time*

Custom Achievement GUI

There might be times when you will want to customize the appearance of your achievement system to match the custom GUI in your App or game. As we saw with leaderboards in the previous chapter, we have the ability to work with the raw data and present it in whatever fashion we choose. This section focuses on adding achievements to your app using your own GUI. As with the leaderboard section, the first thing that we need to do is to add a new button to get to our custom achievement progress view. Add a new button and associated action, as shown in Figure 4-11.

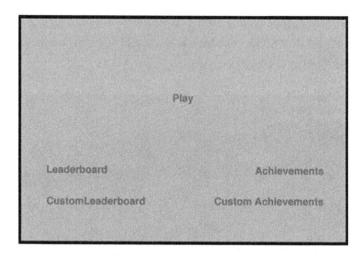

Figure 4-11. *Adding a custom achievement button in Xcode*

We will need to create a new class to handle processing and displaying the achievement progress information. Create a new class named UFOAchievementViewController, and make it a subclass of UIViewController. Set up actions and outlets in the storyboard for a table view, a navigation bar, and a dismiss button. Don't forget to set the data source and delegate for the table view as well.

We also want to create an array that will be used to hold onto the achievement data. Create a new NSArray object and name it achievementArray. We also want to import the GameCenterManager header and conform to its protocol.

Now, hook up the action to present our new UFOAchievementViewController class. Edit the action that was created in UFOViewController to reflect the following changes:

```
@IBAction func customAchievementButtonPressed() {
    let achievementViewController =
    UFOAchievementViewController()
    achievementViewController.gcManager = gcManager
    present(achievementViewController, animated: true)
}
```

Let's take a minute to switch over to the file for UFOAchievementViewController. We need a dismiss action; add that function as well.

```
@IBAction func dismissAction() {
        dismiss(animated: true, completion: nil)
    }
```

If you were to run the app now, you should see a plain and boring table view, similar to the one shown in Figure 4-12. In addition, the dismiss button should now be working.

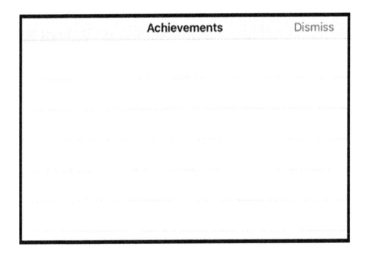

Figure 4-12. *The blank custom table that we will be using for our custom achievements*

Before we can go on with our UFOAchievementViewController, we need to move back into our GameCenterManager class. Add the following method as an optional protocol to the GameCenterManagerDelegate:

```
func achievementDescriptionsLoaded(_ descriptions:
[GKAchievementDescription]?, error: Error?)
```

Then add the following new method to the implementation of
GameCenterManager:

```
func retrieveAchievmentMetadata() {
    GKAchievementDescription.loadAchievementDescriptions {
    (descriptions, error) in
        if let error = error {
            print("An error occurred while loading
            achievement descriptions: \(error.
            localizedDescription)")
        }
        DispatchQueue.main.async {
            self.delegate?.achievementDescriptionsLoaded(
            descriptions, error: error)
        }
    }
}
```

This function will return all the GKAchievementDescriptions that
are found on the Game Center server. We can now move back to our
UFOAchievementViewController class and finish implementing the
custom achievement table.

Important   The retrieveAchievementMetadata function will return
hidden achievements as well. If you want to hide these from the user,
you will have to filter them out of the results.

In addition, add the new protocol that we created earlier. If we do not
encounter any errors, we simply set the returned descriptions to our local
array. When we get the new data, we will also want to refresh the table to
show the data to the user.

```
func achievementDescriptionsLoaded(_ descriptions:
[GKAchievementDescription]?, error: Error?) {
    if error == nil {
        achievementArray = descriptions
    } else {
        print("An error occurred when retrieving
        the achievement descriptions: \(error?.
        localizedDescription ?? "")")
    }
    achievementTableView.reloadData()
  }
}
```

For our numberOfRowsInSection method, we simply return the count on the achievementArray, as follows:

```
func tableView(_ tableView: UITableView, numberOfRowsInSection
section: Int) -> Int {
        self.achievementArray?.count ?? 0
    }
```

We also need to implement a cellForRowAtIndexPath method. Add the following method to the implementation as well. After it is added, we will look at it in more detail:

```
static let tableViewCellIdentifier = "Cell"

    func tableView(_ tableView: UITableView, cellForRowAt
    indexPath: IndexPath) -> UITableViewCell {
        var cell = tableView.dequeueReusableCell(wi
        thIdentifier: UFOAchievementViewController.
        tableViewCellIdentifier)
```

```swift
    if cell == nil {
        cell = UITableViewCell(style: .default,
        reuseIdentifier: UFOAchievementViewController.
        tableViewCellIdentifier)
        cell?.selectionStyle = .none
    }

    let achievementDescription =
    achievementArray?[indexPath.row]

    if let percentage = gcManager?.percentageCompleteOfA
    chievement(withIdentifier: achievementDescription?.
    identifier) {
        cell?.textLabel?.text = (achievementDescription?.
        title ?? "")
    }

    achievementDescription?.loadImage(completionHandler: {
    (image, error) in
        if image != nil {
            cell?.imageView?.image = image
        } else {
            cell?.imageView?.image =
            GKAchievementDescription.
            placeholderCompletedAchievementImage()
        }
    })

    return cell!
}
```

The first half of this function is rather standard; we create a new table cell or we use one from our reusable collection. We are using the default built-in table cell to save some time as well. We create a new GKAchievementDescription and populate it based on the row number from our achievementArray.

The first property we work with is the title, which we use to set the textLabel of the cell. In most circumstances, you will want to use the achievedDescription or unachievedDescription as well as the title. For the sake of simplicity, we use only the title here. Next, we need to set the image for the achievement. This is slightly more complex.

GKAchievementDescription has an image property associated with it, which is nil until you populate it. First, check to see whether the property is populated; we can accomplish this with a simple nil check. If it is populated, we set the cell image to the one that we have cached. If not, we need to load an image from the Game Center servers. To populate it, we call loadImageWithCompletionHandler on the GKAchievementDescription object. This returns the earned image. Notice that we used the default placeholder image, which we can access through a class method on GKAchievementDescription.

Tip   When setting an image in the UITableViewCellStyleDefault cell, do not set the image to nil. This will cause the cell to left align the text and remove the image view. If we then use our block to load the image, it wouldn't appear until the cell or table has been reloaded. This is the reason we set the placeholder image first.

If we were to run the app and visit our custom achievement view, it should look similar to the one shown in Figure 4-13.

Figure 4-13. *Achievement data, as displayed in a custom GUI*

We are able to view only a list of achievements and associated images, but not how far the user has progressed toward unlocking the achievements. If you recall, earlier in this chapter, we wrote a few convenience functions, which can be useful here. We have two functions that will return just the progress for the achievement, percentageCompleteOfAchievementWithIdentifier: and achievementWithIdentifierIsComplete. In addition, if we want access to the entire GKAchievement object, we can use achievementForIdentifier. Let's use the percentageCompleteOfAchievementWithIdentifier: to display the percentage complete here. Modify the section of code in the cellForRowAtIndexPath: that sets the text label of the cell. The new code snippet should look like the following:

```
if let percentage = gcManager?.percentageCompleteOfAchievement(
withIdentifier: achievementDescription?.identifier) {
    let percentageCompleteString = String(format: " %.1f%%
    Complete", percentage)
    cell?.textLabel?.text = (achievementDescription?.title ??
    "") + percentageCompleteString
}
```

If you run the game again, you will notice a more helpful output, as
shown in Figure 4-14.

Figure 4-14. *Achievements with custom GUI and completion*
percentage

Recovering from a Submit Failure

You as the developer are solely responsible for handling achievement-
submitting failures. You do not want your users to lose any achievement
progress. Losing an achievement is very frustrating to your users and
should be avoided at all cost. To prevent this, take the same approach that

we used when working with score failures. The primary difference is that there is no need to store the GKAchievement object because it does not contain any date information or time-sensitive information. We just need to store the percentageComplete. We will create a new method to handle this behavior for us. Add the following method to the GameCenterManager class:

```swift
func storeAchievementToSubmitLater(_ achievement:
GKAchievement) {
        let defaults = UserDefaults()
        let savedAchievementsKey = "savedAchievements"
        var achievementsDictionary = defaults.
        dictionary(forKey: savedAchievementsKey) as? [String:
        Double] ?? [:]

        let achievementKey = achievement.identifier
        let achievementProgress = achievement.percentComplete
        let storedProgress = achievementsDictionary[achievement
        Key] ?? 0

        if achievementProgress > storedProgress {
            achievementsDictionary[achievementKey] =
            achievementProgress
            defaults.setValue(achievementsDictionary, forKey:
            savedAchievementsKey)
        }
    }
```

This function will treat an achievement as an argument and verify whether it is not already stored as a reference in our achievements that have failed to be properly submitted. If it has, then we need to see which one is progressed further so we do not have any instances in which we delete a user's progress. Once that is done, we store it into userDefaults as a dictionary, using the identifier as the key and the percentage completed as the value. We add a call to this method from an error in the submitAchie vement:PercentComplete: function.

Tip   I recommend informing your users their achievement could not be submitted at this time, but it has been saved and will be submitted later. This lets the user know that any progress has not been lost.

We also need a new function that will check to see whether we have uncommitted achievement progress. There is no right answer for when it is a good time to call this function. You can typically get away with calling it after a user authenticates with Game Center, but you may want to add additional methods that it is called from, such as whenever the reachability status is updated. Add the following method to your GameCenterManager class:

```
func submitAllSavedAchievements() {
        let defaults = UserDefaults()
        let savedAchievementsKey = "savedAchievements"

        if let achievementsDictionary = defaults.
        dictionary(forKey: savedAchievementsKey) as? [String:
        Double] {
            achievementsDictionary.forEach { key, value in
                submitAchievement(key, percentComplete: value)
            }

            defaults.removeObject(forKey: savedAchievementsKey)
        }
    }
```

This function loads a copy of our unsubmitted progress and loops through each item, attempting to resubmit them as they go. In the event that they fail to be submitted again, they will be added back to our saved data.

Summary

You now have all the tools you need to add rich and complex achievements into your Game Center–enabled iOS, Mac, or Apple TV app. You now know the value of adding achievements, as well as how to set up and configure them in the App Store Connect portal. We have discussed the pros and cons of using both Apple's default GUI and a custom GUI that you have designed. You now know how to expand our GameCenterManager class to include posting achievement progress, getting achievement feedback, and resetting achievement progress all together.

The most important step completed in this chapter is expanding the reusable GameCenterManager class, which will allow you to easily add achievements in future projects. In the next chapter, we will explore Game Center's matchmaking and invitation systems so you can add multiplayer capabilities and other networking features.

CHAPTER 5

Matchmaking and Invitations

Beginning with this chapter, and through the next few chapters, we will discuss how to add networking and multiplayer capabilities with Game Center, and later GameKit, into your app or game. Adding networking capability to your app is almost considered essential technology in the modern era. Virtually all modern software has some sort of networking component associated with it today, whether it is talking to an online service to retrieve or post information or talking directly to a peer device to exchange data.

In the following chapters, we will discuss communicating with other peer devices, although not all of our networking configurations will be direct peer to peer (see Chapter 6 for details on network design).

This chapter, in particular, explores how to use Game Center to find and invite peers into your app using Game Center's integrated invitation system.

Game Center provides an amazingly undervalued marketing and distribution tool to the developer for very historically low overhead, in regards to handling invitations. When inviting local or Internet users to begin a multiplayer experience in your game or app, you have the option to invite any of your Game Center friends. If the friends that you invite do not currently have the app installed, they will be prompted to purchase the app instantly and begin playing. Even after a decade of Game Center, there

© Kyle Richter and Beau G. Bolle 2022
K. Richter and B. G. Bolle, *Beginning iOS Game Center and GameKit*,
https://doi.org/10.1007/978-1-4842-7756-0_5

are no other methods on iOS to send a "buy now" link to another user in this manner. This functionality provides a great way to grow your user base—just let your users do the selling for you.

Why Add Matchmaking and Invitations to Your App?

When looking at the list of the top ten selling PC or console games for any recent year, you will find it heavily dominated by games that demonstrate a strong focus on multiplayer interaction. Let's take a quick look at the number one selling PC game for 2021, *Call of Duty: Black Ops Cold War*. While this game does feature a single-player mode, this is considered more of an add-on to the game as opposed to the primary selling point. The focus was obviously the multiplayer gaming, even at the sacrifice of the single-player campaign. In recent years, the industry's focus has shifted from creating rich and in-depth single-player campaigns to putting more effort into the multiplayer. There is a perfectly reasonable answer for this new phenomenon: you get more bang for the buck with multiplayer. This is not to say that it is safe to ignore single-player gaming either; there is a growing demand for single-player and couch co-op games.

Humans are, by their very nature, social creatures. We crave social interaction for healthy mental development. Video games and other social software are increasingly becoming an outlet for that interaction. Whether you agree with the sociology of that statement is not what is important here, but the fact remains that multiplayer games are becoming more and more popular. Software users have grown increasingly fond of multiplayer interaction, be it a massive multiplayer online role-playing game or your garden variety first-person shooter with an Internet lobby.

Adding a multiplayer element to your game can increase user playtime by a hundredfold. If you need proof, look at *Quake III Arena* or *Unreal Tournament*, both of which were released in 1999 and both of which still had users logging in for many years after; there is even an active community to this day more than 20 years later. If these games had focused solely on single player, they most likely wouldn't have had such a devoted fan base. Outlined here are some additional reasons why adding matchmaking and invitations through Game Center should be a simple business decision for your products regardless of what platform you are considering:

- Adding a multiplayer component to a game is a great way to add additional polish. Depending on the type of game you are working with, it might be very minor additional work to add a multiplayer element.

- Users have come to expect multiplayer from top-notch games on the App Store.

- You can justify a higher selling point if you have a well-done multiplayer component.

- There is no better way to have users download your app on the fly than the auto-buy invitation system. If you can set up perspective users for a situation in which they are invited to play and can purchase immediately, you will have a much better chance of closing the sale; those new users will bring in more users themselves.

- You can increase playtime or use time in your app or game if you are using an ad-supported system. This will result in more income. If you are selling a paid app, users will feel like they have gotten more value for their money.

- Humans like to compete, so encourage your users to do what they enjoy. Multiplayer might not be for everyone, but for many, it is all they are interested in when shopping for a new game.

Tip   Whenever possible, also provide your users with a single-player option for your game, as there is still a noticeable user base that prefers single-player campaigns.

Common Matchmaking Scenarios

Before we begin working with matches and invitations themselves, it is important to understand some of the scenarios that you might encounter in your quest to implement multiplayer networking into your iOS app or game:

- The first, and probably most common, scenario that you could encounter would be players who are already in your app and want to create an auto-matched game. Both players will already have the app installed and loaded, as well as be in a place where it is expected that they will want to begin a networked session with each other. The invitee player will receive a notification asking whether they want to join a game with the inviter. When both agree, the matchmaking GUI is dismissed and a new match is created.

- Another common scenario that you could encounter would be if the user creates a new matchmaking event and invites other players from their Game Center friends list. The invited friends will receive a push notification informing them that they have been invited to a game; if they already have the game installed and accept the invitation, the game will be launched. Once all invited players have entered the match, the game will begin. If they do not yet have the game installed, they will be prompted to install it, and it will automatically be launched after it has been successfully installed.

- A slightly different event path would occur if a friend is invited and they do not yet have the app installed and have decided to install the app. After the installation process, the app will automatically launch, and you can continue with the normal flow of the matchmaking event.

- A player can also create a new matchmaking event from within the Game Center App itself. In this scenario, all players are launched into the app and receive an invitation to join the match. The best part about this scenario is that if your app already supports invitations, you don't need to write any additional code to support this scenario.

- A player can also invite a friend or multiple friends and fill any remaining slots with the auto-matcher. This is a mix and match of the first two scenarios, and if support for both of them is added, you shouldn't have any additional programming to implement for this scenario.

- The last scenario you could encounter (optionally) is to programmatically auto-match players. In this case, a request would be sent to the Game Center servers and matches would be returned for you. The player would not see any standard GUI and you have the option to implement your own interface.

Note   Matchmaking can only be done between two of the same apps. If the bundle identifier doesn't match, the apps will not be able to communicate over the matchmaking system.

Creating a New Match Request

To create a new match, you first have to create a new GKMatchRequest object. This object represents the desired parameters for the new match that you will be creating. A GKMatchRequest is used both when presenting a GUI and when creating matches programmatically. When working with the GUI, you will pass the GKMatchRequest object to a new instance of GKMatchmakerViewController; on the other hand, if you are handling the matchmaking programmatically, you will pass the object to an instance of GKMatchmaker. See the following sections for more details on programmatic match interaction. For the time being, let's focus on how to create a new match request in your code. Take a look at the following code snippet:

```
let request = GKMatchRequest()
request.minPlayers = 2
request.maxPlayers = 2
```

This example is the simplest demonstration of how to create a new match. You must specify the maximum as well as the minimum number of players. In this example, we are creating a new request that will require exactly two players.

A GKMatchRequest also has a property titled playersToInvite, in which you can use an array of GKPlayer identifiers to automatically populate into a new match. This can be very helpful when playing multiple games that are chained back-to-back and you want to keep the same groups of players together. This property is also prepopulated when your app is launched from the Game Center.app with the players that invited you into the app.

Note   When accepting an invite to a match with a friend, the event is handled from the Game Center App and the playersToInvite property will be populated.

GKMatchRequest also has additional two properties that you will be working with in later sections of this chapter. These are playerAttributes and playerGroup. These two properties are discussed in length in the sections that share their names.

Note   If you are using Game Center as your server for hosting games, you are limited to a maximum of four players. However, if you implement your own server as discussed in the "Using Your Own Server" section of this chapter, you can include up to 16 players.

Presenting Match GUI

We begin with the easiest path forward first, by working with the standard matchmaking GUI provided to us by Apple. Start by first adding a new button to handle presenting the view on the main screen of our test game. I have also gone ahead and renamed the old Play button to Single Player and created a new button called Multiplayer (see Figure 5-1). We will use the UFOViewController to act as the delegate for our matchmaking behavior, so set the view controller to conform to GKMatchmakerViewControllerDelegate. Additionally, modify the action function of the multiplayer button we just added to match the following code:

```
@IBAction func multiplayerButtonPressed() {
    let request = GKMatchRequest()
    request.minPlayers = 2
    request.maxPlayers = 2

    guard let matchmakerViewController = GKMatchmakerViewContro
    ller(matchRequest: request) else {
        print("There was an error creating the matchmaker view
        controller.")
        return
    }

    matchmakerViewController.matchmakerDelegate = self
    present(matchmakerViewController, animated: true)
}
```

We create a new instance of GKMatchRequest, as we did in the previous section. Our demo game will consist of exactly two players, so we set both the max and the min to two.

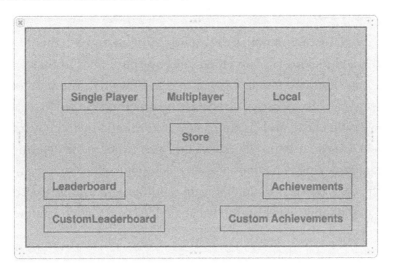

Figure 5-1. *Adding a new button for multiplayer in the UFOViewController storyboard*

In the next part of the code snippet, we create a new instance of GKMatchViewController with the GKMatchRequest we just created.

We also set the delegate to our UFOViewController class. When that is done, we present it as we present any other modal view. You should have output that looks similar to that pictured in Figure 5-2.

If you haven't already done so, now would be a good time to populate your friends list on your sandboxed Game Center account. It is helpful to have several unused email addresses available for this process, as you don't want to use any email addresses that have previously been used with iTunes Connect or with Game Center. Once you have populated a friend or two, you can go ahead and tap on the Invite Friend button pictured in Figure 5-2. You should now see a list of your friends and have the ability to invite them into your app, as shown in Figure 5-3.

Reminder   Do not use any email addresses you have previously used in iTunes Connect or Game Center when creating sandboxed accounts, as it can cause strange and unexpected behavior.

Tip   Many email providers allow you to add a + to the end of your email address to act as an alias. For example, GameCenterRocks@Gmail.com and GameCenterRocks+new@Gmail.com both go to the same inbox, but Apple will treat them as two different email addresses.

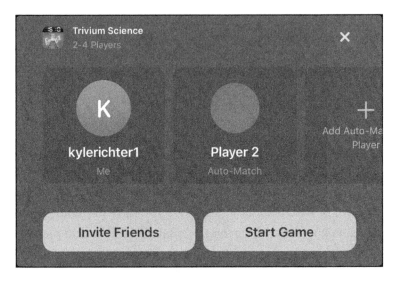

Figure 5-2. *MatchmakerViewController creating a new match GUI with two players*

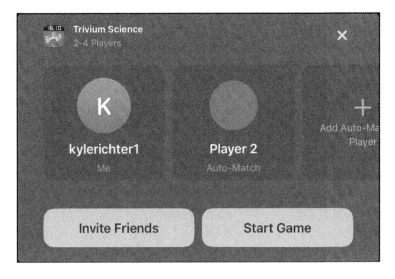

Figure 5-3. *Inviting a friend from your Game Center friends list*

Before we can continue, we need to implement the required delegate functions for the GKMatchmakerViewController. We need to implement the following three functions before we can continue working with matchmaking:

```
func matchmakerViewControllerWasCancelled(_ viewController:
GKMatchmakerViewController) {
    dismiss(animated: true, completion: nil)
}

func matchmakerViewController(_ viewController:
GKMatchmakerViewController, didFailWithError error: Error) {
    dismiss(animated: true, completion: nil)

    let alert = UIAlertController.init(title: "", message:
    "An error occurred: \(error.localizedDescription)",
    preferredStyle: .alert)
    let defaultAction = UIAlertAction(title: "Dismiss", style:
    .default, handler: { action in
        self.dismiss(animated: true, completion: nil)
    })

    alert.addAction(defaultAction)
    present(alert, animated: true, completion: nil)
}

func matchmakerViewController(_ viewController:
GKMatchmakerViewController, didFind match: GKMatch) {
    dismiss(animated: true, completion: nil)
}
```

The first two methods handle user cancellations and failures, while the third method handles the successes. The last method will return a GKMatch object upon success; we will use this object in the following chapters to begin a new match.

133

When working with a variable number of players allowed per match, the user will have the option of adding and removing player slots from the matchmaker view controller as seen in Figure 5-4. When inviting friends into a Game Center match, you will have the option of supplying a short message to be displayed with the invitation, as seen in Figure 5-5.

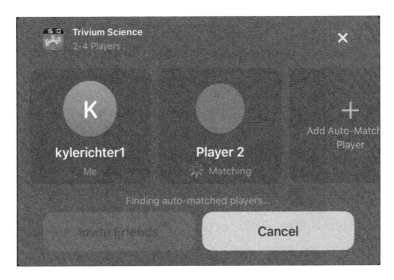

Figure 5-4. *A matchmaker screen with a variable number of players*

Figure 5-5. *Sending an invitation method to a friend asking them to begin a match with you. This message will be sent as an iMessage*

Handling Incoming Invitations

When implementing matchmaking into your app, you also have to implement a system to handle invitations from friends. The invitee's device will receive a push notification informing them that one of their friends has invited them to play a game. Assuming they have the game installed and accept the invitation, you will be required to handle connecting the two players together via a new match. If the invitee does not have the game or app installed, they will be prompted to download it. After the download is finished, the normal invitation process is followed.

Note   You will also need to process invitations from new matches created within Game Center. You most likely won't need to write any additional code; however, you do want to thoroughly test this interaction path.

We will process invitations using an invitation handler (special thanks to Apple for the naming). two distinct delegate methods of the GKInviteEventListener protocol will handle the invite process.

Important   When working with the sandboxed mode and invitations, there can be some quirkiness. If you find yourself never getting the invited push notification, open up the app on both devices and invite the other player on both devices. After this has been done once, it normally restores the ability to test invitations from the springboard.

Now that we know what kind of parameters that we will be working with, as well as the scenarios that we will encounter, we can begin to write a new invitation handler. To keep things clean and simple, we wrap our invitation handler in its own method in our GameCenterManager class. Add the following new method to GameCenterManager:

```swift
public func player(_ player: GKPlayer, didAccept invite:
GKInvite) {
    guard let matchmakerViewController = GKMatchmakerViewContro
    ller(invite: invite) else {
        print("There was an error creating the matchmaker view
        controller.")
        return
    }

    matchmakerViewController.matchmakerDelegate = self
    present(matchmakerViewController, animated: true)
}

public func player(_ player: GKPlayer,
didRequestMatchWithRecipients recipientPlayers: [GKPlayer]) {
    let request = GKMatchRequest()
    request.minPlayers = 2
    request.maxPlayers = 2
    request.recipients = recipientPlayers

    guard let matchmakerViewController = GKMatchmakerViewContro
    ller(matchRequest: request) else {
        print("There was an error creating the matchmaker view
        controller.")
        return
    }
    matchmakerViewController.matchmakerDelegate = self
    present(matchmakerViewController, animated: true)
}
```

Let's break down these functions to see exactly what is happening at each step of the process. The first thing we do is create the GKMatchmakerViewController with the incoming invite object. The delegate for the matchmaker is set to self and the interface is presented to the user.

Important   You cannot accept or otherwise process an invitation formally until you have authenticated a local user with Game Center. It is, therefore, important to register an invitation handler as soon after a successful authentication as possible.

Because we want this to be called as soon as possible after authenticating with Game Center, we add a call to our new method after we have successfully authenticated. Modify the processGameCenterAuthentication method of UFOViewController to match the following one:

```
func processGameCenterAuthentication(_ error: Error?) {
    if let error = error {
        print("An error occurred during authentication:
        \(error.localizedDescription)")
    }
}
```

Tip   If you don't have two devices to test invitations on, you can use the simulator as one of the devices. Don't forget to sign in to the simulator and your device from two different Game Center accounts, or you won't be able to invite each other.

We will use self (UFOViewController) as the delegate for our invitation handler. If you completed the required delegate calls in the last section, "Presenting Match GUI," you will not need to make any additional changes to this class.

Congratulations! You can now handle incoming invitations to your app. In the next section, we will explore how to configure auto-matching to populate invitees for you.

Note   The buy now feature of invitations cannot be tested in the sandboxed environment; it can be used only in live apps. The app must be installed on every device being used in order to test invitations while in sandbox.

Auto-Matching

Auto-matching is a great feature provided to you for no extra work when working with Game Center. Game Center keeps an online queue of people who are waiting to join a multiplayer game in your app. If you do not fill up a new match request with all invited friends, the auto-matching feature will automatically populate the remaining spots with other unmatched players online.

Keep in mind that auto-matching is only as useful as your game is popular; if you do not have a large enough player base to support auto-matching, users will try to join a game for a few moments then exit out when they aren't matched.

You can filter down the auto-matched results using player groups and player attributes, which will be discussed later in this chapter. In addition, you can query the activity of any live player group to see what the average wait time is to be paired up with a new match; this is also discussed more in a later section.

Matching Programmatically

It is also possible for your app to find matches programmatically without using the matchmaker interface. You could use this methodology to implement your own custom GUI for matchmaking or create an "instant match" type action, in which users are automatically paired and a game begins with no additional user interaction. We will not be using this style of matchmaking in our demo app, but the following method will allow you to implement a match programmatically:

```swift
func findProgrammaticMatch() {
    let request = GKMatchRequest()
    request.minPlayers = 2
    request.maxPlayers = 4

    GKMatchmaker.shared().findMatch(for: request,
    withCompletionHandler: { match, error in
        if let error = error {
            print("An error occurred during finding a match: \
                (error.localizedDescription)")
        } else if let match = match {
            print("A match has been found: \(match)")
        }
    })
}
```

The preceding is fairly straightforward. We create a new GKMatchRequest and set the minimum players to two, as well as set the maximum players to four. We then call a new method, `findMatch,` and pass in a copy of our new GKMatchRequest object. This will call our block when a match is found, so it might be a good idea to provide an activity indicator if a match isn't returned quickly. After you have a GKMatch, you can begin a new multiplayer game, as discussed in the following chapters.

When working with programmatically added matches, it is important to allow users a way to cancel the match request if it is taking too long or if they have changed their minds. That action can be accomplished with the following line of code:

```
GKMatchmaker.shared().cancel()
```

Adding a Player to a Match

There might be occasions in which you will want to add a new player to a match after it has already been created. For example, maybe you have a player drop from a game and want to replace him without starting the game over, or a player fails to connect after a game starts and you want to substitute in a replacement. The following function will automatically add a new player to the match using the auto-matching behavior:

```
func addPlayer(to match: GKMatch?, with request:
GKMatchRequest?) {
    if let match = match, let request = request {
        GKMatchmaker.shared().addPlayers(to: match,
        matchRequest: request, completionHandler: { error in
            if let error = error {
                print("An error occurred during adding a player
                to match: \(error.localizedDescription)")
            } else {
                print("A player has been added to the match")
            }
        })
    }
}
```

After a player has been added to a match, you will need to sync that player up with the current match. Adding a player will now allow the player to receive and send data, but they will not have any access to data that has already been sent through the match.

Reinvites

Game Center has the ability to automatically try to reinvite a disconnected player. This method is only supported in two-person Game Center matches. The following function is called when a player is disconnected; Game Center will automatically try to reconnect to that player. If successful, you will receive an additional call to **match(_:player:didChange:)**:

```
func match(_ match: GKMatch, shouldReinviteDisconnectedPlayer
player: GKPlayer) -> Bool {
    true
}
```

Player Groups

Player groups allow you to specify different classifications for each player. Game Center, by default, auto-matches everyone into the same group. With player groups, you can specify that certain players are looking for groups that contain only other players of that group.

For example, players who want to play a certain level of dungeon or a specific race track will be grouped together, so they are paired up with other people who want to play that same level. Player groups can be used to segregate players into many different types of groupings, such as the following:

- Players who wish to play the same level of a map (such as a race course), area in an RPG, map in a first-person shooter, or level in an action game.

- Separate players based on skill level. Either have players choose the skill level that they wish to play at, or automatically determine their skill level based on past performance or previous win streaks.

- Type of game that is being played. For example, players can be broken down into who wants to play Capture the Flag, Team Deathmatch, Domination, or Last Man Standing.

- Players of the same Clan, Guild, Team, or Network who want to play together.

- Players who have purchased additional in-app content and can no longer be paired up with those who do not have the same content available for any reason.

A player group isn't restricted to these items and can be used to group players together in whatever fashion meets the needs of your app. A player group is represented by the playerGroup property on a GKMatchRequest. The only restriction placed on this property is that it must be represented by an Int. Specifying a playerGroup is rather straightforward, as seen in the following code snippet:

```
let myForestMap = 123456789
let request = GKMatchRequest()
request.minPlayers = 2
request.maxPlayers = 4
request.playerGroup = myForestMap
```

Under most circumstances, you will want to let your users select the playerGroup that they belong to; however, there might be instances in which this is not true, such as automatically determining a player's skill level.

Caution   After you set playerGroup to any nonzero value, players will only be matched with other players of that group.

Player Attributes

Like player groups, player attributes are used during matchmaking to narrow down the possible available games to the user. Player attributes, which generally function the same as player groups, do handle some things in a different manner. Some of the many uses for player attributes include the following:

- Often, in role-playing games, characters pick a class. It is common to require a group of multiple classes—such as a healer, a fighter, and a mage—in order to complete a quest.

- Sports games often have various positions on a team, such as goalkeeper, fullback, midfielder, and forward. A team will require a mix of all of these to be able to play.

- In a submarine simulator game, you could also have various players, such as a captain, sonar operator, pilot, and weapons systems.

- In a first-person shooter game, you could need players in roles such as close-quarter combat specialist, sniper, medic, and platoon leader.

Understanding Player Attribute Limitations

Player attributes can be used to assign these values to each player so that you can balance a team that contains the required players. However, there are a number of limitations when using player attributes; it is important that you familiarize yourself with them before you begin working with player attributes:

- Only a single player may fill a role. For example, you cannot require three midfielders in a soccer game.

- All roles must be filled before the game is considered ready to start. For example, you can't have a first-person shooter without a sniper (based on the preceding example).

- Each player can fill only one role at a time; players cannot offer to join a game in a position that would fill more than one role. For example, you couldn't have a player in a first-person shooter willing to play either a sniper or a medic; they will need to pick one before the match request is finalized.

- Player attributes are used during auto-matching. If you invite a friend into a game, they are not tested to see whether they match the role that needs to be filled. Instead, they will automatically be assigned a random, unassigned role. In short, friends do not get to pick their player attributes.

- Roles are not displayed anywhere in the standard matchmaking graphical user interface. You will need to implement your own system prior to entering this view to allow users to select their roles.

- The GKMatch object does not contain information about which players have been assigned which roles. You will need to implement your own system after the match is connected to determine who is playing which role.

- There is no system in place to determine which roles are overfilled or which are harder to find matches for. For example, everyone might want to play a mage in a role-playing game and no one might want to be a healer; therefore, it would be much harder for a mage to find an open game, while a healer can easily find one.

Working with Player Attributes

Don't let the long list of limitations scare you off from player attributes. Even with the listed limitations, they can be extremely valuable in creating a better multiplayer experience. Let's look at an example of how to build a match using player attributes:

```
struct PlayerClass: OptionSet {
    let rawValue: UInt32

    static let squadLeader      = PlayerClass(rawValue:
                                    0xFF000000)
    static let breacher         = PlayerClass(rawValue:
                                    0x00FF0000)
    static let grenadier        = PlayerClass(rawValue:
                                    0x0000FF00)
    static let lightMachineGun = PlayerClass(rawValue:
                                    0x000000FF)
}
```

We begin by defining a mask for each of our player attributes, which we will refer to as "classes" for the rest of this section. This example represents a standard squad in a modern military-style game. Each class is assigned a different value of a mask. Game Center uses an algorithm to match these players together, using the following rules.

- A match's mask will always begin with the mask of the inviting player.

- Game Center will ignore all players who have not set a player attribute mask if the inviting player has set a player attribute mask.

- A player will be added to a match only if their player attribute mask doesn't overlap any section of a mask from any players already invited into the match.

- After adding a player to the match, the value of that player's attributes value is logically OR'ed into the match's mask.

- If a match's mask value is equal to FFFFFFFFh, then the match is considered complete and can begin; if the mask does not equal FFFFFFFFh, then Game Center will continue searching for a player who can fill the match.

- There is no way to query Game Center to see which player is still currently being waited on.

The following is based on the classes we just defined.
A blank match will have the player attribute mask shown in Figure 5-6.

Figure 5-6. *An empty player attribute mask (0x00000000)*

Player 1 begins a new match and selects Squad Leader as his class. When that player creates the match, it will now have a player attribute mask that looks like that shown in Figure 5-7.

Figure 5-7. *A player attribute mask representing the Squad Leader class (0xFF000000)*

Now the creator of the match uses Game Center to auto-match for new players. The first player Game Center finds has selected a class of Grenadier. The Grenadier will have a mask, which looks like that shown in Figure 5-8.

Figure 5-8. *A player attribute mask representing the Grenadier class (0x0000FF00)*

When compared to the already existing match's mask, as shown in Figure 5-9, we can see there are no overlaps, so that player can be invited into the game.

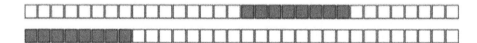

Figure 5-9. *Comparison of 0xFF000000 and 0x0000FF00*

When these masks are combined to form the new match mask, it will look like that shown in Figure 5-10.

Figure 5-10. *A new match mask, representing two players (0xFF00FF00)*

Player 3 selects Breacher as his class and searches for a game. Game Center finds the match that we have been working with and determines that there is room for a Breacher by comparing the match's mask to the Breacher's mask, as shown in Figure 5-11.

Figure 5-11. *The top is the current match's mask (0xFF00FF00), and the bottom is a Breacher's mask (0x00FF0000)*

Since there is no overlap between the masks, the Breacher can be invited into the game. Player 4 selects the class of Grenadier and has Game Center look for a match. Game Center again will find our match in progress and attempt to add the new player to it.

Since the mask supplied by Player 4 overlaps a part of the match's mask (see Figure 5-12), that player is not allowed to join. If Game Center cannot find an open match for that player, then it will begin looking for new players to fill in the holes on that player's match.

Figure 5-12. *The top is the current match's mask (0xFFFFFF00), and the bottom is a Grenadier mask (0x0000FF00)*

Player 5 selects Light Machine Gun as his mask and begins looking for a game to join. Game Center compares his mask to the current match's mask, as shown in Figure 5-13.

Figure 5-13. *The top is the current match's mask (0xFFFFFF00), and the bottom is a Light Machine Gun's mask (0x000000FF)*

Since there is no overlap between the two mask sets, Player 5 can join the match. This will create a complete player attribute mask for the match, as shown in Figure 5-14.

Figure 5-14. *A completed match mask (0xFFFFFFFF)*

If Player 5 never joined the game, and the original inviter wanted to fill the slot with a friend from Game Center, the invited friend would not have an option to select his class. The match, in that case, would have a mask that looks like that shown in Figure 5-15. The invited friend would then be assigned the mask, shown in Figure 5-16, that would complete the match's mask. This would complete the player attribute masks and allow the game to begin.

Figure 5-15. *The current match's mask (0xFFFFFFF0)*

Figure 5-16. *A Machine Gun's mask (0x000000FF), needed to complete the match's mas*

Setting a player attribute is very straightforward and is shown in the following code snippet:

```
struct PlayerClass: OptionSet {
    let rawValue: UInt32

    static let squadLeader     = PlayerClass(rawValue:
                                     0xFF000000)
    static let breacher        = PlayerClass(rawValue:
                                     0x00FF0000)
    static let grenadier       = PlayerClass(rawValue:
                                     0x0000FF00)
    static let lightMachineGun = PlayerClass(rawValue:
                                     0x000000FF)
}
...
let request = GKMatchRequest()
request.minPlayers = 4
request.maxPlayers = 4
request.playerAttributes = PlayerClass.squadLeader.rawValue
```

Player Activity

Game Center provides a method to query for recent player activity. Your users will often want as much information as possible about how long of a wait they could experience while looking for a multiplayer match. It is important to establish that player activity is recent activity and not current activity. There is no Apple-provided method for determining exactly how many players are waiting for a match, but Apple does provide a way to determine how many users have recently looked for a match. Let's take a look at the required source code to get player activity. Add the following two new functions to your GameCenterManager class's implementation file:

```
func findAllActivity() {
    GKMatchmaker.shared().queryActivity { activity, error in
        DispatchQueue.main.async {
            self.delegate?.playerActivity?(activity as
            NSNumber, error: error)
        }
    }
}

func findActivityForPlayerGroup(_ playerGroup: Int) {
    GKMatchmaker.shared().queryPlayerGroupActivity(playerGroup)
    { activity, error in

        let activityDictionary = [
            "activity": activity,
            "playerGroup": playerGroup,
        ]

        DispatchQueue.main.async {
            self.delegate?.playerActivity?(forGroup:
            activityDictionary, error: error)
        }
    }
}
```

We also need to add two new protocol methods to GameCenterManagerPlayerDelegate in GameCenterManager.swift. Add the following two functions:

```
func playerActivity(_ activity: Int?, error: Error?)
func playerActivity(forGroup activityDict: [AnyHashable :
Any]?, error: Error?)
```

When you implement these new protocol methods in your UFOViewController as follows:

```
func playerActivity(_ activity: Int?, error: Error?) {
    if let error = error {
        print("An error occurred while querying player
        activity: \(error.localizedDescription)")
    } else {
        print("All recent player activity: \(activity ?? 0)")
    }

}

func playerActivity(forGroup activityDict: [AnyHashable :
Any]?, error: Error?) {
    if let error = error {
        print("An error occurred while querying player
        activity: \(error.localizedDescription)")
    } else {
        if let activity = activityDict?["activity"],
            let playerGroup = activityDict?["playerGroup"] {
            print("All recent player activity: \(activity) For
            group: \(playerGroup)")
        }
    }
}
```

you should get output similar to the following:

```
2021-03-08 11:11:04.007 UFOs[3000:207] All recent player
activity: 3 For Group: 12345 2021-03-08 11:11:04.008
UFOs[3000:207] All recent player activity: 3
```

So now that we have player activity for a specified player group, what do these numbers mean? Apple has never specified the exact meaning of these numbers, but through careful research, it appears that they represent the number of users who attempted to connect to a game using the auto-matching feature in the last one to three minutes. The numbers seem to reset at an undeterminable interval somewhere within that time frame. In addition, there appears to be a 15–30 second delay until new numbers are reflected from users attempting to join a match.

Even with the limitations imposed by player activity, it can still be a very valuable tool in determining possible wait times for your users to find a match. However, you want to make sure these numbers are used for informational purposes only, as they tend to be just unreliable enough to depend upon.

Note   You can implement your own server system to keep track of exactly how many players are waiting for a match if the Apple system does not provide specific enough information on player activity for the needs of your app.

Using Your Own Server (Hosted Matches)

Under normal circumstances, Game Center will host your match for you; however, Apple has provided a technique for implementing your own server to host a match. This approach is called a "hosted match" and can be implemented in any app to add increased flexibility to Game Center-based multiplayer networking.

When using Game Center to host a match, every device that is connecting to that match creates an instance of GKMatch. The GKMatch class does all the legwork of connecting, handshaking, sending and receiving data, and handling errors. However, there are times when you will need to implement your own server, most notably if you want to allow more than four people to connect to a single match at a time. In this scenario, you can use Game Center to find peers for your match and use your own server to connect those peers.

Tip   Using a hosted match allows you to connect up to 16 users, as opposed to the limit of four while using Game Center hosting.

There are several downsides to using your own server, however, most notably that you are now responsible for all the legwork that was previously given to you for free by Game Center, specifically the following:

- You must design and implement all of your own networking code to connect the peers together. Game Center will find the matches for you, but its involvement stops there.

- If your app is using the standard matchmaking interface, your server must inform the app when a new peer successfully connects so that it can update the GUI.

We will need to make a handful of minor changes to our code base in order to support hosted matches on the device side. We begin by modifying our multiplayer button action method that we set up earlier in this chapter.

```
@IBAction func multiplayerButtonPressed() {
    let request = GKMatchRequest()
    request.minPlayers = 2
    request.maxPlayers = 4

    guard let matchmakerViewController = GKMatchmakerView
    Controller(matchRequest: request) else {
        print("There was an error creating the matchmaker view
        controller.")
        return
    }

    matchmakerViewController.matchmakerDelegate = self
    matchmakerViewController.isHosted = true

    present(matchmakerViewController, animated: true)
}
```

As you can see, we added a new line, `matchmakerViewController.isHosted = true`, which tells the matchmaker GUI that this match will be hosted on our own servers. In addition to setting the matchMakerViewController to hosted, you will need to have each device connect to your server. This section does not deal with how to code the server itself, as there are dozens of languages and approaches that can be taken here. However, after a device has connected to your server, it needs to call the following with the player who is joining:

```
matchmakerViewController.setHostedPlayer(player, didConnect:
true)
```

This will update the GUI on all the connected players' screens, informing them that a new player is ready to begin a match. After all the players are connected to your server, and have confirmed that they are ready, your delegate is called to begin the game. When working with Game

Center matches, we used the delegate callback **matchmakerViewContro
ller(_:didFind:)** to begin a match. However, for a hosted game, we use the
following:

```
func matchmakerViewController(_ viewController:
GKMatchmakerViewController, didFindPlayers playerIDs: [String]) {
    dismiss(animated: true, completion: nil)
    print("Players: \(playerIDs)")
    //Begin Hosted Game
}
```

At this point, you can begin the game with your server handling the
communication between the connected players. In addition, you can
begin a hosted match programmatically, as we saw with a Game Center-
hosted match earlier in this chapter.

```
func findProgrammaticHostedMatch() {
    let request = GKMatchRequest()
    request.minPlayers = 2
    request.maxPlayers = 16

    GKMatchmaker.shared().findPlayers(forHostedRequest:
    request) { players, error in
        if let error = error {
            print("An error occurred during finding a match:
            \(error.localizedDescription)")
        } else if let players = players {
            print("Players have been found for match:
             \(players)")
        }
    }
}
```

As you can see, it is very similar to our previous method; however, instead of getting back a GKMatch object, we are returned an array of players. You will also note that we can also increase the maximum players to 16.

Summary

In this chapter you were introduced to the concepts of matchmaking and invitations. We discussed the overwhelming benefits of adding multiplayer to your iOS, Mac, or Apple TV app or game, as well as some of the hurdles you might need to jump along the way. We explored the matchmaking process from presenting the standard Apple GUI to highly customized matches using player groups and player attributes. We reviewed how to process invitations in every possible scenario, as well as how to query for player activity. Finally, we discovered how it is possible to implement your own server to remove some of the limitations placed on Game Center. We expanded our reusable Game Center Manager to handle matchmaking, invitations, and the required overhead so that you can quickly add multiplayer ability to your apps.

In this chapter, we deeply explored how to create matches and populate them with peers. In the upcoming chapters, we will not only learn how to communicate between the peers but also explore new methods for locating peers with whom to communicate. The next chapter covers information on how to design a Network Environment for use with your game or app.

CHAPTER 6

Network Design Overview

In the previous chapters, we learned how to find and establish connections to peers through a variety of methods using both Game Center and GameKit. In this chapter, we will look at how to design a networking experience for a modern computer game. This chapter is written and laid out slightly different than the previous chapters you have encountered in this book. Primarily, there will be no associated source code with this chapter, and we will only briefly touch on GameKit networking topics themselves. This chapter will focus on the concepts of network design from an academic viewpoint, as opposed to actually implementing the network itself. In the next chapter, you will discover how to tie everything together and have your peers begin to communicate with each other.

While it is entirely possible (and all too often performed) to go ahead and just start writing your network logic without any planning or forethought, it is probably not a great idea. After all, you wouldn't begin writing a new app or game without first planning out how the logic of it will function. Network design is a complex topic, and you should approach it with a plan; otherwise, you could find yourself rewriting the entire system from scratch after putting a lot of work and effort into it. You don't want to find yourself up against a wall because the approach you took limited your options for future expandability. Just like with software, you shouldn't

© Kyle Richter and Beau G. Bolle 2022
K. Richter and B. G. Bolle, *Beginning iOS Game Center and GameKit*,
https://doi.org/10.1007/978-1-4842-7756-0_6

jump right into writing code on the first day. You should whiteboard things out a little and get a feel for the requirements of the project.

Take, for example, a desktop role-playing game called Clan Lord that was written in the late 1990s for the Mac. Clan Lord has maintained a very dedicated fan base that has kept the game active and continual to the present day. However, when the game was originally written, many network-related issues were seemingly not properly thought through for a game that would still be played more than two decades later.

Clan Lord uses frame-by-frame syncing for all of its network calls. This means that every frame, every element visible on the player's screen, has to be transmitted. This approach works and works well while you have a small game, a small user base, and limited complex functionality. However, when you are designing software, you cannot have a limited vision for the future. Always plan for the best or, depending on your perspective, the worst case. When designing a network, you must take into account what you will want to do six months, a year, or even ten years from now with your game or app. It is all too often that software far exceeds its estimated life span and continues to operate well beyond when its initial software developers had intended; we need to look no further than the Y2K bug to see this in action. Every developer assumes something better will be along shortly to replace the work they are doing; more often than not they are wrong and products live on long past when it makes practical sense to keep them going.

Clan Lord now suffers from long-ingrained problems, such as a five frames per second rendering engine, due to the fact that you cannot sync more than five full frames of data per second on the average home network. This could have been prevented by implementing some logic into the client when the project was first started; for example, it would have been much more efficient to inform the client where objects are and when they move, as opposed to fully syncing everything in each frame. In addition, player movement is limited to four to five frames per second because actions have to be synced back to the server, making it hard to react to events. This also could have been prevented by using prediction algorithms, discussed later in this chapter, to determine where a player will end up during movement.

Clan Lord is one example of a game that was much more popular or at the very least had a much more dedicated fan base than planned and lived a lot longer than anyone expected. Sadly, when this happens, you are limited to the vision and design that you had when the project was first started. It is much harder to undo something later than to do it initially. When designing your network, take time to do it carefully and intentionally, as it can haunt you and your app for a very long time.

Three Types of Networks

Although there are many different types of network designs in existence, there are three practical and primary kinds of networks that you can implement when designing your network infrastructure. Picking a primary type of network is a good place to start, as it will guide you toward the next step in the design process.

We will be focusing on just these three of the primary types of network designs, but keep in mind that there are dozens of other well-known network configurations, some of which we will briefly touch on in this section. The three types of networks we will be discussing in length throughout this chapter are peer-to-peer, client-to-host, and ring networking.

Peer-to-Peer Network

A peer-to-peer network (see Figure 6-1) is the most common network that you will see on the iOS/Mac platform. No device is treated any differently than any other device, and each device is in charge of sending and receiving data to all the other peers it wishes to communicate with. While this type of network may look complicated, it is one of the most simple and straightforward approaches to joining together multiple devices in communication.

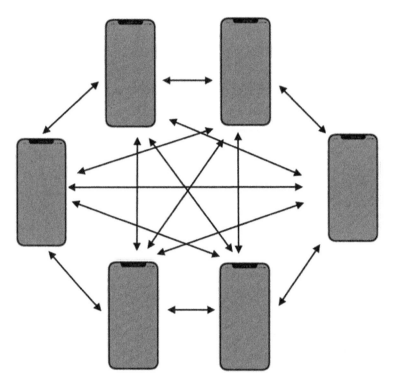

Figure 6-1. *A visual representation of a peer-to-peer network using six iOS devices*

A peer-to-peer network is commonly used when dealing with Game Center networking because it is the easiest to implement on the platform. While this approach has the benefit of being extremely easy to set up, it has an equal number of weaknesses. Primarily, it can cause a lot of redundant overhead. Each peer needs to inform every other peer about its actions. In a six-way network like the one shown in Figure 6-1, this means that each device needs to send out five messages every time it wants to update the game state. In addition, if you are implementing a system in which each peer confirms a successful message, you will also need to receive five messages to confirm each event.

Another disadvantage of a peer-to-peer network is that it can become very confusing to work with a large number of peers. As you can see from Figure 6-1, things can get messy quickly. Unlike the other primary types of networks that we will discuss in this section, the peer-to-peer approach is the only one without a clear flow. Each peer can message any other peer, by definition. This also means that you have to keep track of what every peer needs to know. Under most circumstances, this is a perfectly acceptable approach. However, when you begin to deal with more complex types of networks and information that needs to be sent and received, this configuration might no longer be ideal.

In addition, no one device is in control of the state of the game. If there are artificial intelligence components, then you will need to figure out a system that will allow them to stay in sync between all the devices.

Client-to-Host Network

A client-to-host network designates one device to be the host, or server if you prefer that terminology. This device is responsible for sending information to all the connected clients. The clients never speak to each other; they speak only to the host who then relays the required information back to the other clients. An example of what a client-to-host setup looks like is shown in Figure 6-2.

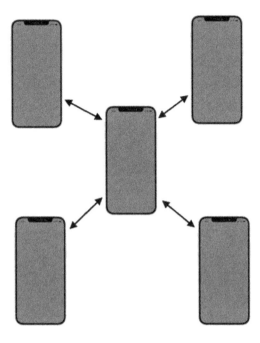

Figure 6-2. *A visual representation of a client-to-host network using five iOS devices*

A client-server network simplifies the flow of data. Each peer or client only needs to worry about itself and the host; they do not need to be aware of the other devices that might exist on the network. The benefit of this type of network is that one device keeps everything in sync and handles the flow of information; this makes it a very secure network (in the sense of anti-cheating). Cheating, however, is not a large concern on the iOS platform because it's a sandboxed system to begin with; the state of the Mac is a little more open, but often it is not a major concern until a game becomes very successful.

There are other benefits to this system as well, such as the fact that only one device needs to worry about the state of the network, and that sole device is in charge of the behavior of the network. This type of network simplifies events such as connections, disconnections, transmission errors, and other state changes such as computer-controlled objects like artificial intelligence. However, this same setup could be troublesome on the iOS platform; if the host device has too much information to process, that device could run slower or use more battery. This approach also requires two separate logic handlers, one for the client and one for the host. This type of system becomes a dedicated server system in larger environments when one player is no longer needed to be the host.

Ring Network

A ring network (see Figure 6-3) has no host and no clients. It works similarly to a peer-to-peer network, but a peer is in charge of communicating with only one designated peer and will receive information from only another separately defined peer. The information flows through a group of devices in the shape of a ring, hence the name.

This type of network isn't very common on the iOS platform, as there is not a lot of argument for the redundancy that it typically provides for disconnected peers. Apple has done a lot of the groundwork to ensure that networks remain active and stable, without the need for the developer to spend additional design hours ensuring that there won't be instances where peers lose contact with other peers that are currently joined together. There are times, however, where you might find this type of configuration useful when designing your network on the iOS platform. Keep in mind as you add additional clients to a ring network that the time it takes for information to complete a circuit of the ring increases and can be especially bogged down by one or more laggy devices.

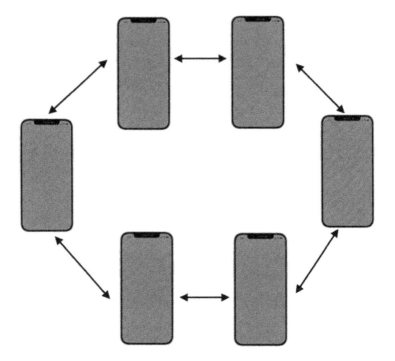

Figure 6-3. *A visual representation of a ring network using six iOS devices. Notice how much simpler this diagram appears than the peer-to-peer network shown in Figure 6-1*

Less Common Networks

There are many additional types of network designs available in computer science. Some are more practical than others, and some are mostly theoretical. In this section, we cover some of the better known "uncommon" networks. Although some of these can be implemented on iOS devices, most will likely not have any real benefit for the average project:

- Headless Client: The client has no data whatsoever and is controlled by a host device. You can think of this type of setup as a computer terminal that is booted from a server disk.

- Dedicated Server: The host in this example does not participate in the game or activity and is dedicated to sending the information out from the peers and collecting new input. This is typically seen deployed by large companies creating a gaming community. A dedicated server system can be seen as an extension of the client to host setup where the host becomes a dedicated machine.

- Mesh/Partial Mesh Network: This is a peer-to-peer network in which each peer may not be aware of the other peers that exist on the network. The packets are tagged with a destination and every hop attempts to get the packet closer to the destination. A full-mesh network means that every peer is interconnected, which is more or less the same as a peer-to-peer network practically speaking.

- Tree Network: This type of network consists of a tree of peers interconnected to each other and each controlled by a centralized point. The central point passes messages to other central points, and each tree branch passes messages back and forth along that branch.

- Hybrid Network: This type of network combines two or more technologies, such as two groups of peers who are linked together through a centralized server.

This covers most of the networks you will encounter during a career of software engineering. There is really no limit to the type of network that you can design, and every year better designs and flows become available. If you find this topic especially interesting, there are many great resources available online that dive into network design in much greater detail. In the next section, we will look at the actual packets that will be sent and received on your network.

Reliable Data vs. Unreliable Data

When dealing with network design, packet reliability is an important topic. When discussing packet reliability, we are specifically referring to the priority of the data, the ordering of the packets, and the retry determination factor. Let's look at all these attributes separately and how they relate to network design (see Table 6-1) before we dig into the specifics we need for our implementation when dealing specifically with the Apple platforms.

Table 6-1. *Common Packet Attributes and How They Affect Network Behavior*

Attribute	Relationship to network design
Priority	When you are working with low-level networking, you are dealing with packets. Each packet is a predetermined size and contains information about the event that you want to send to another peer. Packets are typically sent to a queue and then sent out to the peer they are addressed for, but because networking isn't precise (especially if you are trying to get the lowest latency), packets might not always be received in the order that they are generated.
	For example, in a standard online game, you might be passing two types of information, game state changes, and chat information. Obviously, your character requesting an action, such as attacking an enemy or dodging an attack, is more important to have in a timely manner than a chat message.
	The solution to this type of problem is to set priority for packets. The peer will send cycle through all its pending messages and send the highest priority ones first. This allows the vital messages to be retried in the event of failure first, as well as bump the important packets to the top of the queue.

(continued)

Table 6-1. (*continued*)

Attribute	Relationship to network design
Ordering	The order in which packets are received can be crucial. For example, if you are sending 10 packets, which together make up a very long chat message, or together make up the game state, then the order in which those packets are received is important to the receiving peer.

If the packets aren't received and processed in order, your message could appear scrambled. When this happens with a state engine, very unpredictable behavior may follow. There is a certain cost overhead involved when ensuring packets are ordered, however. If you are waiting for packet 1 of 10, then you can't do anything with the packets you might have already received. This creates a situation in which your network is only as fast as your slowest packet. If ordering isn't critical to your network functioning correctly, then you should not worry about the order. Remember that maintaining order is expensive; only require it where it is actually required. |

(*continued*)

Table 6-1. (*continued*)

Attribute	Relationship to network design
Retry	Networks are, by nature, unreliable. Even a desktop machine hooked up to a dedicated connection will have lost packets and experienced other failures. When you are dealing with network reliability on a mobile device, the only thing you can reliably count on is failure. When you send a packet to another peer, you can handle it two ways: the first is a send-and-forget system; the second is a send-and-verify system.
	In the first approach, you send a packet and you don't really care if it gets there. Let me clarify: you do care, but if it fails, there is nothing you can do about it. A good example of this type of acceptable failure is a voice chat packet. If it fails to reach the end of the line successfully, resending it will merely bring things out of sync; it is better to just continue on streaming the data. The result of course will be a brief loss of voice but it's better than the alternative.
	In the second approach, the packet is considered vital, such as player opening a chest, searching a slain foe for treasure, or updating their direction of movement. The peer needs this data to be sent to continue smoothly executing the commands. If you skip this packet, it will be frustrating to the user, as they will have to retry the action themselves instead of having the network retry it for them.

Now that we have covered the issues that are important when dealing with sending the actual data packets from one device to another, we can look at how these principles apply to the Apple platforms themselves.

There are two types of modes that data can be sent in with GameKit: the first is GKSendDataReliable; the second is, naturally, GKSendDataUnreliable. Let's take a look at what each one of these modes do for us and how they fit in with the topics we just discussed. See Table 6-2.

Table 6-2. *Packet Attributes and How They Apply to Game Center*

Attribute	GKSendDataReliable	GKSendDataUnreliable
Priority	GameKit networking doesn't factor in any type of priority when dealing with packets. Packets are sent in the order that they are fed into the system.	GameKit networking doesn't factor in any type of priority when dealing with packets. Packets are sent in the order that they are fed into the system.
Ordering	Packets will be received in the order that they are sent.	Packets using this method are not guaranteed to be received in the same order that they were sent.
Retry	A packet will be continuously retried until it is successfully received. The next packet will not be sent until the first one has been confirmed received.	A packet is sent and then removed from the queue. The API does not wait to receive a received notification before it sends the next packet. This is naturally faster than waiting for a response between each packet.

Sending Only What Is Needed

One of the vital mistakes that first-timers make when designing a network is sending too much data. It is easy to just send everything. In the beginning of this chapter, we talked about a game that exhibited this very problem.

If I had more time I would write a shorter letter.

—Blaise Pascal

171

Pascal could have very well been talking about network packets, in this often-misattributed quote. The size of the packet can be directly related to the speed, stability, and scalability of your network. It is important to spend the time to figure out what the absolute bare minimum is that can be sent. It is also likely worth the time to figure out how to condense the data you do have.

Take a look at a hypothetical example that some of you might encounter while designing a game. For this example, let's say you are working on a role-playing game. You control your hero and guide them through a series of dungeons. In these dungeons, you can interact with items and encounter various enemies, which you will fight in real time.

Well, we know we will have some static data; for example, the layout of the dungeon probably will not be changing while you are inside it, so instead of sending the map tiles to the client every frame or even periodically, we should send that data when the player first enters the zone. There might be elements that will be moving, but we can predict their behavior infinitely, such as a river flowing or a torch flickering. These items can also be loaded once with the information they need to stay in sync. Also consider whether it's important that these items are even in sync with the server; a torch flicker might not need to be in sync on every client at once.

There are, of course, items that will need to be updated throughout the player's adventures in the dungeon. The player themselves will need to be updated every time the user performs a new action. For example, if you are running east, you could send a packet every frame to tell the server that you are running east. However, a much more efficient way to handle this interaction is to tell the server to begin moving east at full speed. When you are done moving east, you should inform the server that you want to stop. This type of interaction drastically reduces the number of messages that need to be sent to the server to accomplish the same task. Optimizations such as these is why, when playing modern games, you sometimes see disconnected players running into walls—the server never received a stop-running command before the client disconnected. These same optimizations are why you will sometimes see a very lagged player jumping around in a bunch of different directions.

Take the time to carefully design how you will structure your network data. You can always add more information, but it becomes very difficult to remove data as you dig deeper into your network design. Always look for a way to reduce packet size, as there is no downside to packets being too small, but a packet that is too large will cause you a lot of suffering down the road.

Prediction and Extrapolation

Let's take another example into consideration: this time, a racing game. Each player controls a car that is guided around a track. We know where each car is at the start of the race. We also know that any messages we send to the server will have an inherited latency due to the round-trip network time. Should we not update the car positions until the server tells us to? That would result in a very choppy racing game. To account for this very common issue, we use predictive technology.

We know that race cars will, more than likely, continue on a current course for the next handful of frames. We will assume things will continue doing what they are doing until the server tells us otherwise; if the user steers slightly to the left or right, that is a minor correction we will need to make when the server informs us of the update. The fact that an object in motion will stay in motion until acted on by an outside force is not just a law of physics; it is also the first rule of designing a predictive network.

The chances of an object completely reversing its current course are much less likely than slightly modifying its current course. This makes it easier to account for minor changes if the server informs you that things are out of sync. In the event that a player does completely change direction or otherwise break your prediction about what actions were going to continue, you are only off the mark by as much as your current latency, which is typically only a small fraction of a second. If you have an object that is likely to continue doing what it is doing—such as a player moving, objects in a falling state, bullet trajectory, or any type of physics simulation—the best bet is to continue assuming that those actions will continue until the server informs you that they have changed.

Formatting Messages

Whenever you are dealing with designing a network for a game or game-like application, you are guaranteed to be dealing with at least two types of messages. These are often referred to as state messages and server messages. A state message is a message that will directly affect your game engine, such as a player moving or opening a chest. Server messages deal with the glue that holds everything together, such as connections, disconnections, pings, and errors.

It becomes important to quickly sort these messages to different handlers. It is a good design pattern to keep the parsing of these messages in different places. After all, you don't want to be scanning all your chat messages in a first-person shooter for client timeout messages. There are many different methods to handle this segregation, but I have found a simple prefix is suitable for most cases. If you prefix all of your state messages with a character that you will not see in server messages, you can quickly check the first character in incoming messages to make sure they are delivered to the correct parser. If you are designing a more complex network, you can use a large number of possible prefixes to make sure things get to the correct place. In Chapter 8, we will look at practical examples of message formatting when we begin to send and receive data.

Preventing Cheating and Preventing Timeout-Related Disconnections

One thing that has not become a big concern on the iOS platform, as of yet, is cheating through network exploits. Likewise, the Mac App Store has remained relatively free of cheating and abuse. If you are an online gamer, you are probably all too familiar with this behavior. A clever user will determine how the network behaves and then send commands that the client itself would never send, such as increase hit points to max float or decrease respawn time to zero. Although you might need to have your server respond to things such as increase or decrease hit points, you want to make sure the server is in control. For example, instead of letting the client say "increase moment speed to fifty," you should set up the message to something like "request increase moment speed" and then have the server return the new speed. If you put clients in charge of variables, at some point someone will take advantage of this and exploit your system. When thinking through your network design, the best practice is to never trust the client to tell you the truth about the game state. You will want to remove as much dependance as possible on the client's version of events or state of the world.

If your client doesn't have any updates to send out to the server or its peers, it is good practice to send a message that simply states, "I'm still here, don't disconnect me," which is known as a "keep alive" message. Although you don't have to worry about timeout disconnection on the GameKit platform, it is still a good idea to make sure that you keep your own line of communication open between idle peers.

When you are designing a message architecture, you can really think of it as designing an API; there are a lot of similarities, and you have to follow the same guidelines. If you ship version one of your app with a command that lets users query for their movement speed, you can't easily pull out that command in version two because previous clients might still be depending on it. Follow the same guidelines that API developers do: test everything thoroughly because after it is out in the wild, it is very hard to get it back.

What to Do When All Else Fails

An issue that is bound to come up when you have been working with networks long enough is that of what to do when the system you have designed no longer meets your needs. Let's discuss something that might be familiar to those of you who have taken some logic or business courses. There is a syndrome known as the "sunk cost fallacy," where when dealing with nonrefundable resources, such as time, those costs are weighed as equally as refundable costs.

Take a look at the following equation:

$$\text{Payoff} = \text{project revenue} - \text{open cost}$$

Now let's look at the same example using some real-world data. In 1968, Knox and Inkster approached 141 horse bettors: 72 of the people had just finished placing a $2.00 bet within the past 30 seconds, and 69 people were about to place a $2.00 bet within the next 30 seconds. The hypothesis was that people who had just committed themselves to a course of action would reduce post-decision dissonance by believing more strongly than ever that they had picked a winner. Knox and Inkster asked the bettors to rate their horse's chances of winning on a seven-point scale. What they found was that people who were about to place a bet rated the chance that their horse would win at an average of 3.48, which corresponded to a "fair chance of winning," whereas people who had just finished betting gave an average rating of 4.81, which corresponded to a "good chance of winning." This hypothesis was confirmed: after making a $2.00 commitment, people became more confident that their bet would pay off. Knox and Inkster performed an ancillary test on the patrons of the horses themselves and managed to repeat their finding almost identically.[1]

What we are talking about is accepting when it is time to give up and start over. Giving up is never a popular solution; our brains are wired against it. We look at the nonrefundable cost and calculate that into our favor. Once you have already made an investment, it is easier to justify that investment and try to defend it. No one wants to be the person to call it quits and throw away all the time and money already invested into a project; however, when you spend time and resources on a development project, they are spent and they cannot be recouped. You cannot justify more time simply based on time spent.

There is no right answer on when to give up and start over, and there is no wrong answer. The only thing you can do is look at the problem objectively. If you hadn't already invested into this problem, what solution would you pick?

The best approach is to always think through architecture decisions before implementing anything. However, it is all too often that developers spend time trying to fix something instead of starting over. With networking it is easy to build out a design, but it is much harder to change and readapt an existing solution. Sometimes the best course of action is to wipe the slate clean and begin anew.

Summary

In this chapter, we looked at the design of the actual network, as opposed to the platform-specific information that we have dealt with in the rest of this book so far. You could easily design a working network without the information in this chapter, through common sense and gut instinct, but

---

[1] Knox, R. E., & Inkster, J. A. (1968). "Postdecision dissonance at post time." *Journal of Personality and Social Psychology, 8,* 319–323

keep in mind the lesson learned throughout this chapter: just because it works doesn't mean it works well. Designing a network is easy; designing a network correctly is very difficult.

There is significantly more information on network design than can easily fit into a single chapter, or even a single book. If I can leave you with a final piece of advice: when you begin to look at how to structure your network, think through everything as you go, and never feel the need to be satisfied with your first solution.

In the next chapter, we will finally get to work with sending our messages from one device to another. Chapter 9 will also be an extension of that technology where we look into how to add voice chat services to your app.

CHAPTER 7

Exchanging Data

In a previous chapter, we explored how to connect to peers through a variety of methods. So far, we have not been able to do much with that connection. In this chapter, we will learn all that there is to know about exchanging data between sets of peers using GameKit and Game Center networking. We have already added the ability to find peers using Game Center to our UFO game. We will now add the ability to actually play a multiplayer match.

Because all the groundwork has already been laid out in the previous chapters, there are only two items that we need to worry about in regards to exchanging data. First, we need to send the actual data; second, we need to receive and process that data on the other side. Everything else that you need to do is already done, except some logic for disconnecting. Let's jump right into it by modifying our source code from Chapter 5.

Modifying a Single-Player Game

There are a few modifications that we need to make to our single-player game in order to transform it into a multiplayer game:

- Once we connect to a new peer, we need to begin the game. We also need a way to inform our existing engine that the new game is multiplayer.

© Kyle Richter and Beau G. Bolle 2022

K. Richter and B. G. Bolle, *Beginning iOS Game Center and GameKit*, https://doi.org/10.1007/978-1-4842-7756-0_7

- One device needs to be designated the host device. We will have this one device control the movements of the cows, since both devices can't control cow movement themselves. This is an important step if we want both devices to appear in sync.

- Each peer needs to inform the other peer(s) about its actions, such as movement and tractor beam usage.

- Each peer needs to parse the other peer's device and update its own game state to keep both devices in sync with each other.

These steps are a representation of the bare minimum that is typically required to turn a single-player game into a multiplayer game. Your particular game or app might be much more complex. For example, your multiplayer experience might be so different from your single-player gameplay that you cannot reuse the same class for both modes. On the other hand, your game might be even simpler. For example, a multiplayer game of Battleship wouldn't require either device to be the host because there are no computer-controlled elements that you need to worry about keeping track of.

Setting Up Our Engine for Multiplayer

The very first thing that we need to do is let our game engine know whether the state should be set to multiplayer or single player. There are complex ways and simple ways of doing this. Depending on your needs, you will most likely be able to get away with a simple state variable.

A state variable is the approach that we will use for our example, since our game is extremely straightforward. In UFOGameViewController.swift, we create a new property to represent a Bool, which will be set to inform the class whether we are in single-player or multiplayer mode. Add the following lines into our already existing file:

```
class UFOGameViewController: UIViewController {
    var gameIsMultiplayer = false
}
```

We will use this property throughout our code base to determine whether the game is running in multiplayer mode.

We have an existing function in UFOViewController that will be called when our game begins a new multiplayer match. Game Center returns a GKMatch object to help us identify the game. We will also add some new methods in our GameCenterManager class to handle communication to this system. For now, we will simply focus on getting the game up and running in a new state.

```
func matchmakerViewController(_ viewController:
GKMatchmakerViewController, didFind match: GKMatch) {
        dismiss(animated: true, completion: nil)
}
```

Next, we add a section of code to the end of this function to begin a new multiplayer game after we find a peer that we want to play against. Go ahead and add the following snippet of code into each method:

```
let gameVC = UFOGameViewController()
gameVC.gcManager = gcManager
gameVC.gameIsMultiplayer = true

navigationController?.pushViewController(gameVC, animated: true)
```

We also need to hold onto the GKMatch that represents a peer. Create two new properties in the UFOGameViewController, named peerIDString and peerMatch. Set these up in the same fashion that you did for the gameIsMultiplayer property. The new section of your header should look like the following abstracted snippet:

```
class UFOGameViewController: UIViewController {
    //...
    var peerIDString: String?
    var peerMatch: GKMatch?
}
```

Now we need to add logic to set these properties for beginning a new multiplayer game. These functions should now look like the following ones.

When we load our game view controller, we know whether it is multiplayer or not, as well as having a reference to our peer or peers. Our GameViewController now has all the information it needs to begin a new multiplayer game.

```
func matchmakerViewController(_ viewController:
GKMatchmakerViewController, didFind match: GKMatch) {
    dismiss(animated: true, completion: nil)

    let gameVC = UFOGameViewController()
    gameVC.gcManager = gcManager
    gameVC.gameIsMultiplayer = true
    gameVC.peerIDString = nil
    gameVC.peerMatch = match

    navigationController?.pushViewController(gameVC, animated:
    true)
}
```

Picking a Host

Picking which device will be the host is harder than it sounds. Both devices, when first connected together, are treated as equals. How do we then determine which device will have more control than the other?

The most straightforward and foolproof system that I have used is having each device generate a random number. Whichever device has the largest random number becomes the host. In the very rare event that both devices generate the same random number, we simply try and generate two new random numbers again.

After we have determined the random number, a device has picked for its chance at being the host; we need to send that data to the other device. On the other side, we need to process the data and have both devices come to the same conclusion about which one has been selected as the host. This section deals only with generating the host number; the next two sections handle how to send and receive this data. We now add the following function to our UFOGameViewController class:

```
func generateAndSendHostNumber() {
    let randomHostNumber = Double(arc4random())
    let randomNumberString = "$Host:\(randomHostNumber)"

    gcManager?.sendString(toAllPeers: randomNumberString,
    reliable: true)
}
```

For the purpose of this particular example, we will work with a string for sending the data back and forth. You could easily send this as an Int as well, but whatever we send will first need to be converted to data, which we will cover in the next section. In addition, we want to make sure this method is called whenever we are dealing with a multiplayer game.

To do so, we need to add the following to the end of our viewDidLoad method. We also need to slightly modify our logic to spawn cows. If it is a multiplayer game, only the host is responsible for spawning and updating cow paths.

Tip When you begin to deal with more complex networking, it is often beneficial to switch to a data type that can easily store more data with less parsing, such as a dictionary or an array.

```
override func viewDidLoad() {
    //...
    generateAndSendHostNumber()
    if gameIsMultiplayer == false {
    for _ in 0..<5 {
                spawnCow()
            }

            updateCowPaths()
        }
}
```

Sending Data

We will work with two primary functions to send data to other connected peers. One will handle sending data to every peer we are connected to, and the other will send data only to specified peers, such as teammates or other groups of players. First, add the following two methods to our GameCenterManager class:

```
func sendStringToAllPeers(_ dataString: String, reliable: Bool)
func sendString(_ dataString: String, toPeers peers: [String]
reliable: Bool)
```

We will use these functions to send strings back and forth, but you can add additional methods to accept any type of input that you want to work with for your particular game. Keep in mind that everything will need to be converted to data along the way. You might also notice that the first function is the same method we called previously from our generateAndSendHostNumber.

Tip   It is a good idea to implement functions to handle arrays and dictionaries if you plan on building a reusable Game Center class. These are both very common data types when working with networking messages.

Before we can really begin to send data back and forth, we need to know the GKMatch that was created for our multiplayer game. To do this, we create a new property in the GameCenterManager class. We name it matchOrSession and set it to an ID type. We need to set this property before we begin a new multiplayer game, after we have been returned either a new GKSession or GKMatch. Let's first take a look at sending data to all peers. The new method is posted as follows. After you have examined it, we will discuss it in further detail:

```
func sendStringToAllPeers(_ dataString: String, reliable: Bool) {
    guard matchOrSession != nil else {
        print("Game Center Manager matchOrSession property
        was not set, this needs to be set with the GKMatch or
        GKSession before sending or receiving data")
        return
    }
}
```

```
guard let dataToSend = dataString.data(using: .utf8) else {
    print("Game Center Manager dataString could not be
    converted to Data.")
    return
}

var sendError: Error?

if let session = matchOrSession as? MCSession {
    let peers = session.connectedPeers
    let mode: MCSessionSendDataMode = reliable ? .reliable
    : .unreliable

    do {
        try session.send(dataToSend, toPeers: peers,
        with: mode)
    } catch {
        sendError = error
    }
} else if let match = matchOrSession as? GKMatch {
    let mode: GKMatch.SendDataMode = reliable ? .reliable :
    .unreliable

    do {
        try match.sendData(toAllPlayers: dataToSend,
        with: mode)
    } catch {
        sendError = error
    }
} else {
    print("Game Center Manager matchOrSession was not a
    GKMatch or a GKSession, we are unable to send data.")
}
```

```
    if let sendError = sendError {
        print("An error occurred while sending data:
        \(sendError.localizedDescription)")
    }
}
```

We need to make sure that we have properly set the matchOrSession property. If we haven't, we will not be able to continue, as we will be using this object to send data. After we have ensured that we have the proper information to continue, we then transform our NSString to an NSData object. This encodes the string into a format that is safe for sending over the network. We also need to set the reliability mode, as discussed in Chapter 7.

Now that we have everything in place to actually send data, we first detect whether we are working with a GKMatch from a Game Center–type connection or a GKSession from a Peer Picker–type connection. All that is left to do is send the data using the GameKit APIs.

Now is a good time to look at how we will selectively send data only to certain peers. We can build off the example we already have for sending data to all peers. Let's take a look at our sendString function:

```
func sendString(_ dataString: String, toPeers peers: [Any],
reliable: Bool) {
    guard matchOrSession != nil else {
        print("Game Center Manager matchOrSession property
        was not set, this needs to be set with the GKMatch or
        GKSession before sending or receiving data")
        return
    }
    guard let dataToSend = dataString.data(using: .utf8) else {
        print("Game Center Manager dataString could not be
        converted to Data.")
        return
    }
```

```
var sendError: Error?

if let session = matchOrSession as? MCSession, let peerIDs
= peers as? [MCPeerID] {
    let mode: MCSessionSendDataMode = reliable ? .reliable
    : .unreliable

    do {
        try session.send(dataToSend, toPeers: peerIDs,
        with: mode)
    } catch {
        sendError = error
    }
} else if let match = matchOrSession as? GKMatch, let
players = peers as? [GKPlayer] {
    let mode: GKMatch.SendDataMode = reliable ? .reliable :
    .unreliable

    do {
        try match.send(dataToSend, to: players, dataMode:
        mode)
    } catch {
        sendError = error
    }
} else {
    print("Game Center Manager matchOrSession was not a
    GKMatch or a GKSession, or peers was not the correct
    type of array, we are unable to send data.")
}
```

```
    if let sendError = sendError {
        print("An error occurred while sending data:
        \(sendError.localizedDescription)")
    }
}
```

This method is very similar to the method for sending data to all peers. The main difference is that we use a new API call and feed in an array of peer IDs or players. You can, of course, change these methods to accept more than a string when sending data, but for the simplicity of our test game, a string is all we need.

This concludes everything you need to know about sending data between two or more iOS, Mac, or Apple TV devices. In the next section, we will look at how to receive and parse the data we get from another peer.

Receiving Data

GKMatch has its own system for receiving delegate callbacks for incoming data. Game Center uses the same delegate that we used for our invitation handler in Chapter 5. We will begin by modifying that existing function.

The first step in setting up our app to receive data is to set the receive data delegate to our GameCenterManager class. We will use the GameCenterManager class as a filter point for passing data back into our game. While you could easily receive data in your Game Controller itself, if we pipe everything throughout GameCenterManager, it makes it much easier to plug this class into future apps.

Modify both matchmakerViewController of UFOViewController.swift to match the following:

```
func matchmakerViewController(_ viewController:
GKMatchmakerViewController, didFind match: GKMatch) {
        dismiss(animated: true, completion: nil)

        gcManager?.matchOrSession = .match(match)

        let gameVC = UFOGameViewController()
        gameVC.gcManager = gcManager
        gameVC.gameIsMultiplayer = true
        gameVC.peerMatch = match
        navigationController?.pushViewController(gameVC,
        animated: true)
    }
```

The important change to focus on in the preceding function is setting the delegate to handle the incoming data request to our GameCenterManager class. This allows us to handle all incoming data in one centralized place; from there, we can relay it out to the relevant sections of the app.

Next, you need to add the following function to your GameCenterManager class. This new function handles incoming data from Game Center. This function assumes we will be working with only incoming strings because that is the design we have chosen when dealing with sending data in our game. You can easily adapt this method to handle receiving other types of objects. In addition, we will expand this new function to handle game-specific data. You can also further adapt this setup to use a more complex and intelligent system of data parsing, but it will be more than suitable for the needs of UFOs.

```swift
func receivedData(_ dataDictionary: [AnyHashable : Any]?) {
    guard let dataDictionary = dataDictionary as? [String:
    String] else { return }
}
```

Tip   You can use the context property to pass any data to the received delegate method.

Further modify the receivedData function to handle all the possible types of data that will be seen in our game:

```swift
func receivedData(_ dataDictionary: [AnyHashable : Any]?) {

    guard let dataDictionary = dataDictionary as?
    [String: String] else { return }

        determineHost(dataDictionary)

}
```

All that is left now is to implement our function to determine which player is the host; add a new function as seen in the following code snippet:

```swift
func determineHost(_ dataDictionary: [String : String]?) {
    if Double(dataString ?? "") ?? 0.0 == randomHostNumber {
        print("Host numbers are equal, we need to reroll
        them")
        generateAndSendHostNumber()
    } else if Double(dataString ?? "") ?? 0.0 >
    randomHostNumber {
        isHost = true
```

```
        for _ in 0..<5 {
            spawnCow()
        }

        updateCowPaths()
    } else if Double(dataString ?? "") ?? 0.0 <
    randomHostNumber {
        isHost = false
    }
}
```

If you run the game on two devices now, you can see that each log reflects whether the device has been designated a host or whether the other device is the host. The receivedData function is very flawed, though, because it only works with the host data message. In the next section, we will refine this function to accept not only the host message but also input for player movements, cow movements, and other game actions.

You now have all the basic skills required to send data between two different iOS, Mac, or Apple TV devices, as well as receive and parse that data and have your system react to it. If you want to experiment with working with these calls in practice, the next section will walk you through several examples of sending and receiving data in our UFOs game.

Putting Everything Together

In the last section, we learned how to receive the data that has been sent to a device. In this section, we walk through the exercise of actually using received data in a useful way for our game. We add a second player, allow movement information to be sent over the network, sync up state data across both devices (such as cow movement), track each player's score, and complete various other required overhead tasks associated with our particular game.

Selecting the Host

Let's start by improving the host selection logic that was implemented in the previous section. Right now, any data that we receive is assumed to be the host number. Because most of the data we receive will not be the host number, we need to find a way to filter that data to where we can parse it. Modify the generateAndSendHostNumber function to match the following code block:

```
func generateAndSendHostNumber() {
    randomHostNumber = Double(arc4random())
    let randomNumberString = "$Host:\(randomHostNumber)"

    gcManager?.sendStringToAllPeers(randomNumberString,
    reliable: true)
}
```

As you can see, we now add an identifier prefix to the message that we will send. I have chosen for this example the prefix of $Host:, but you can use whatever system you want. In addition, we need to modify the receivedData callback to support the new format.

```
func receivedData(_ dataDictionary: [AnyHashable : Any]?) {

        guard let dataDictionary = dataDictionary as? [String:
        String] else { return }

        if dataDictionary["data"]?.hasPrefix("$Host:") ?? false {
            determineHost(dataDictionary)

        } else {
            print("Unable to determine type of message:
            \(dataDictionary)")
        }
    }
```

If we determine that the message is a host message, we send it to a new helper function called determineHost to determine which device is the host. If we are unable to determine the type of message, we print a warning message to the console, which will help us debug later down the road. We need to move the old code from receivedData into determineHost. In addition to moving the code, we need to strip off the prefix. Although stripping off the prefix has a lot of overhead, it is the easiest way to accomplish this task. In more complex apps, you might need to design a more robust message system.

```swift
func determineHost(_ dataDictionary: [String : String]?) {
        let dataString = dataDictionary?["data"]?.
        replacingOccurrences(of: "$Host:", with: "")

        if Double(dataString ?? "") ?? 0.0 == randomHostNumber {
            print("Host numbers are equal, we need to reroll
            them")
            generateAndSendHostNumber()
        } else if Double(dataString ?? "") ?? 0.0 >
        randomHostNumber {
            isHost = true
        } else if Double(dataString ?? "") ?? 0.0 <
        randomHostNumber {
            isHost = false
        }
    }
```

Now we can still determine who the host is, but we have opened the door to be able to process more than only this type of data.

The next step will be transmitting and displaying our peer's UFO into our game. In this chapter, I have added two new images to the project, EnemySaucer1.png and EnemySaucer2.png. These are the same as the originals but with a different color scheme applied to them. We will use this new artwork to display the opponent's spacecraft.

Displaying the Enemy UFO

The first thing we need to do is detect whether we are a multiplayer game, and if so, we need to draw the enemy UFO in the viewDidLoad function of UFOGameViewController. You will notice this is the exact same code we use for drawing the player in single-player mode except we use a different graphic asset.

```swift
override func viewDidLoad() {
        super.viewDidLoad()

  if gameIsMultiplayer {
            let otherPlayerFrame = CGRect(x: 100, y: 70, width:
            80, height: 34)
            otherPlayerImageView = UIImageView(frame:
            otherPlayerFrame)
            otherPlayerImageView?.animationDuration = 0.75
            otherPlayerImageView?.animationRepeatCount = 99999
            let imageArray = [UIImage(named: "EnemySaucer1.
            png"), UIImage(named: "EnemySaucer2.png")]
            otherPlayerImageView?.animationImages = imageArray.
            compactMap { $0 }
            otherPlayerImageView?.startAnimating()
            if let otherPlayerImageView = otherPlayerImageView {
                view.addSubview(otherPlayerImageView)
            }
        }
}
```

If we were to run the game on two devices and begin a new multiplayer game, we would now see a red enemy UFO that just sits in the sky. The next step is to send our movement data to our peer so that they can update where the enemy player is. To do so, we add a new code snippet to the end of our movePlayer function.

```
func movePlayer(_ vertical: double, _ horizontal: double) {
    //...
    if gameIsMultiplayer {
            let positionString = "$PlayerPosition:
            \(playerFrame?.origin.x ?? 0.0) \(playerFrame?.
            origin.y ?? 0.0)"

            gcManager?.sendStringToAllPeers(positionString,
            reliable: false)
        }
}
```

Here we send your player's x and y coordinates to the peer every time you move. We will be sending the data as unreliable, since if we fail, we can just use the next packet. You may remember back to Chapter 7 that this is one of the benefits of sending the full data instead of the delta of the movement. The data will always be updating while the player is moving.

This would be a great place to use predictive technology, as discussed in Chapter 7, but for simplicity's sake, we will be syncing every frame. In addition, there are better ways to send the x and y coordinates to another device, such as a dictionary or custom data format. However, encoding them into a string is the easiest to understand. As you develop your game or app, you can design this type of function to be more streamlined with less overhead.

Tip   Using stringWithFormat carries with it a lot of overhead. In practice, you should use methods such as stringByAppendingString to further optimize this type of code.

We also need to update our receivedData function to handle the new type of data we are expecting. Modify that function to match the new one as follows. In addition, we add a new function to parse the incoming data. Also add a new function called drawEnemyShipWithData, as follows:

```
func receivedData(_ dataDictionary: [AnyHashable : Any]?) {

    guard let dataDictionary = dataDictionary as?
    [String: String] else { return }

    if dataDictionary["data"]?.hasPrefix("$Host:") ?? false {
        determineHost(dataDictionary)
    } else if dataDictionary["data"]?.
    hasPrefix("$PlayerPosition:") ?? false {
        drawEnemyShip(withData: dataDictionary)
else {

        print("Unable to determine type of message:
        \(dataDictionary)")
    }

    }

func drawEnemyShip(withData dataDictionary: [String : String]?) {
    let dataArray = dataDictionary?["data"]?.
    components(separatedBy: " ")

    let x = Double(dataArray?[1] ?? "") ?? 0.0
    let y = Double(dataArray?[2] ?? "") ?? 0.0

    otherPlayerImageView?.frame = CGRect(x: CGFloat(x), y:
    CGFloat(y), width: 80, height: 34)
    }
```

This function parses the incoming data from the network. We pull the x and y coordinates out of the string that we received, and we update the enemy player's frame with the new position. This type of approach is syncing the two devices frame by frame and is very inefficient. Given more time, this function should be updated to use predictive technology to determine where the player is heading and only update the feed if the player goes against the prediction. However, for the purposes of this demo, it suits our needs. For more information on predictive networking, see Chapter 7.

If you were to run the game now and begin a new multiplayer game, you would see that each device reflects the movement of its partnered device. We still need to spawn the cows, add the tractor beam, and update the scores, but we have a functional (albeit dull, for the time being) multiplayer game, as shown in Figure 7-1.

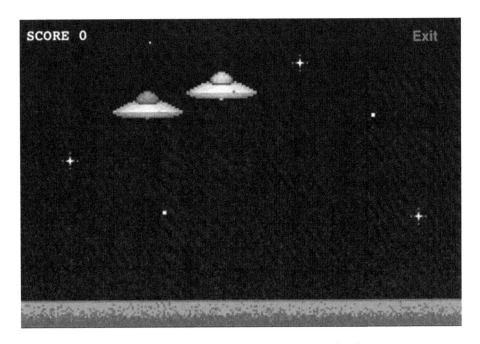

Figure 7-1. *Adding a second player to UFOs. Each player can move around independently and is kept in sync through the network*

Spawning Cows

Because we want the cow movement to be synced between each device, we need to dedicate one device to handling the cow spawning and movement paths. We have already picked a host device, so we will let the host determine where the cows will be placed. We begin by modifying the determineHost function. As you can see in the following code, if we are the host, we begin our normal spawn cow process:

```swift
func determineHost(_ dataDictionary: [String : String]?) {
    let dataString = dataDictionary?["data"]?.
    replacingOccurrences(of: "$Host:", with: "")

    if Double(dataString ?? "") ?? 0.0 == randomHostNumber {
        print("Host numbers are equal, we need to
        reroll them")
        generateAndSendHostNumber()
    } else if Double(dataString ?? "") ?? 0.0 >
    randomHostNumber {
        isHost = true

        for _ in 0..<5 {
            spawnCow()
        }

        updateCowPaths()
    } else if Double(dataString ?? "") ?? 0.0 <
    randomHostNumber {
        isHost = false
    }
}
```

We also need to modify our spawnCow function to support the new networking behavior. All we are doing here is determining whether we are a network game and whether we are the host and then sending the data to our network handlers.

```swift
func spawnCow() {
    let x = Int(arc4random() % 480)

    let cowImageView = UIImageView(frame: CGRect(x: CGFloat(x),
    y: 260, width: 64, height: 42))
    cowImageView.image = UIImage(named: "Cow1.png")
    view.addSubview(cowImageView)
    cowArray?.append(cowImageView)

    if isHost && gameIsMultiplayer {
        gcManager?.sendStringToAllPeers(String(format:
        "$spawnCow:%i", x), reliable: true)
    }
}
```

Modify the receivedData function to support the new $spawnCow message type. We also want to extract the x axis origin from the message and pass it to a new method that will handle spawning a cow from the network. Both of these functions are shown next:

```swift
else if dataDictionary["data"]?.hasPrefix("$spawnCow:") ??
false {

        let x = Int(dataDictionary["data"]?.replacing
        Occurrences(of: "$spawnCow:", with: "") ?? "") ?? 0

        spawnCow(fromNetwork: x)
    }
```

Tip   Our host doesn't need to pass the y axis coordinate for the cows because they are always spawned on the same y axis. If you can eliminate data from a packet, it is always beneficial as this type of unnecessary data adds up.

If you were to run the game now, you would see that both devices spawn cows in the exact same location, but the host device is the only device that animates the cow movements.

The next step is to add the logic to share the animation control for the cows. Modify the existing updateCowPaths method to send the newX and array position of the cow we want to update. The following new code should be added to the end of the for loop:

```
if gameIsMultiplayer {
        let dataString = String(format: "$cowMove:%i:%f",
        x, newX)
        gcManager?.sendStringToAllPeers(dataString,
        reliable: true)
    }
```

Note   Because we set the data for the spawn cow call to reliable, it is guaranteed to be received in the order that it was sent. This means that we can be assured that the objects in our cowArray on both devices will be in the same order.

We also need to add a new data handler to our receivedData function. We pass the entire dictionary to our new updateCowPathsFromNetwork function.

```
else if dataDictionary["data"]?.hasPrefix("$cowMove:") ?? false {

        updateCowPaths(fromNetwork: dataDictionary)
}

func updateCowPaths(fromNetwork dataDictionary: [String :
String]?) {
      let dataArray = dataDictionary?["data"]?.
      components(separatedBy: ":")

      let placeInArray = Int(dataArray?[1] ?? "") ?? 0

      let tempCow = cowArray?[placeInArray] as? UIImageView

      let currentX = Double(tempCow?.frame.origin.x ?? 0.0)

      let newX = Double(Int(dataArray?[2] ?? "") ?? 0)

      if tempCow != currentAbductee {
          UIView.animate(
              withDuration: 3.0,
              delay: 0,
              options: [.curveLinear],
              animations: {
                  tempCow?.frame = CGRect(x: CGFloat(newX),
                  y: 260, width: 64, height: 42)
              }
          )
      }

      tempCow?.animationDuration = 0.75
      tempCow?.animationRepeatCount = 99999
```

```
//flip cow
if newX < currentX {
    let flippedCowImageArray = [UIImage(named:
    "Cow1Reversed.png"), UIImage(named: "Cow2Reversed.
    png"), UIImage(named: "Cow3Reversed.png")]
    tempCow?.animationImages = flippedCowImageArray.
    compactMap { $0 }
} else {
    let cowImageArray = [UIImage(named: "Cow1.png"),
    UIImage(named: "Cow2.png"), UIImage(named: "Cow3.
    png")]
    tempCow?.animationImages = cowImageArray.compactMap
    { $0 }
}

    tempCow?.startAnimating()
  }
{
```

This function is very similar to our existing function for updating cow paths. The two differences are that we get our place in the array from the network, and we don't randomly generate a newX position. If you were to run the game again, you would see that both sets of cows are now in sync with each other. When a cow changes position, it is reflected exactly the same on both devices. Figure 7-2 shows the current state of the game.

Figure 7-2. *Syncing up the cow movements over the network between two iOS devices*

Each player can now abduct cows and increment their score. There are, however, still two remaining issues that need to be addressed. The first is that we don't share scores between devices, and the second is that we don't show the other player's tractor beams or animate the cows into the UFO during the abduction. Let's start off by adding in support for the score.

Sharing Scores

When we increment the score, we send that data to our peers. Add the following snippet of code to our finishAbducting function, right after we increment the score:

```
if gameIsMultiplayer {
        gcManager?.sendStringToAllPeers("$score:\(score)",
        reliable: true)
}
```

We, again, need to modify our receivedData method to support the new $score message. I have chosen to increment the enemy score within the receivedData method. You can, of course, write a new method to handle this functionality. In addition, we need to add a new label for the enemy score. It will be placed directly below the local player's score. Figure 7-3 shows the scores in place.

```
else if dataDictionary["data"]?.hasPrefix("$score:") ?? false {
        let enemyScore = Float(dataDictionary["data"]?.
        replacingOccurrences(of: "$score:", with: "") ??
        "") ?? 0.0

        enemeyScoreLabel.text = String(format: "ENEMY
        %05.0f", enemyScore)
    }
```

Tip Technically, you don't need to pass the score value in with the network call because scores are always incremented by one; we can assume a new score message means increment the value by one.

Figure 7-3. *Adding the score for the networked player*

Exercise   It would be very easy to add logic to declare a winner of the game when either player reaches a score of ten. Try to add this logic into the game yourself.

Adding Network Abduction Code

The last thing that we need to handle is tying in network support for the abduction code. We need to properly remove and respawn cows as they are abducted, as well as show the enemy UFO using their tractor beam and animating a cow into the ship.

Let's begin by showing and hiding the tractor beam on each device. Because we start a tractor beam every time a user touches the screen, and end it when the user releases that touch, we can begin there. We have no values that need to be transmitted; the only thing we need to be aware of is starting and stopping the animation itself. Modify the touchesBegan and touchesEnd methods to send a message to the peer. The modified methods are shown as follows:

```
override func touchesBegan(_ touches: Set<UITouch>, with event:
UIEvent?) {
        currentAbductee = nil

        tractorBeamOn = true

        if gameIsMultiplayer {
            gcManager?.sendStringToAllPeers("$beginTractorBeam",
            reliable: true)
        }

        tractorBeamImageView?.frame = CGRect(x:
        (myPlayerImageView?.frame.origin.x ?? 0.0) + 25, y:
        (myPlayerImageView?.frame.origin.y ?? 0.0) + 10, width:
        28, height: 318)
        tractorBeamImageView?.animationDuration = 0.5
        tractorBeamImageView?.animationRepeatCount = 99999
        let imageArray = [UIImage(named: "Tractor1.png"),
        UIImage(named: "Tractor2.png")]

        tractorBeamImageView?.animationImages = imageArray.
        compactMap { $0 }
        tractorBeamImageView?.startAnimating()

        if let tractorBeamImageView = tractorBeamImageView {
            view.insertSubview(tractorBeamImageView, at: 4)
        }
```

```
    let cowImageView = hitTest()

    if let cowImageView = cowImageView {
        currentAbductee = cowImageView
        abductCow(cowImageView)
    }

}

override func touchesEnded(_ touches: Set<UITouch>, with
event: UIEvent?) {
    tractorBeamOn = false

    if gameIsMultiplayer {
        gcManager?.sendStringToAllPeers("$endTractorBeam",
        reliable: true)
    }

    tractorBeamImageView?.removeFromSuperview()

    if let currentAbductee = currentAbductee {
        UIView.animate(
            withDuration: 1.0,
            delay: 0,
            options: [.curveEaseIn,
            .beginFromCurrentState],
            animations: {
                var frame = currentAbductee.frame

                frame.origin.y = 260
                frame.origin.x = (self.myPlayerImageView?.
                frame.origin.x ?? 0.0) + 15

                currentAbductee.frame = frame
            }
```

```
            )
        }

        currentAbductee = nil
    }
```

As you can see, we simply check to make sure that we have a network game and then pass a message to begin or end the tractor beams. Next, we add a handler to our receivedData function to call two new methods that will display and animate the tractor beam on the peer's device. These two functions are modifications of our current tractor beam animation methods and are shown next for your convenience:

```
func beginTractorFromNetwork() {
        otherPlayerTractorBeamImageView?.frame = CGRect(x:
        (otherPlayerImageView?.frame.origin.x ?? 0.0) + 25, y:
        (otherPlayerImageView?.frame.origin.y ?? 0.0) + 10,
        width: 28, height: 318)
        otherPlayerTractorBeamImageView?.animationDuration = 0.5
        otherPlayerTractorBeamImageView?.animationRepeatCount =
        99999
        let imageArray = [UIImage(named: "Tractor1.png"),
        UIImage(named: "Tractor2.png")]

        otherPlayerTractorBeamImageView?.animationImages =
        imageArray.compactMap { $0 }
        otherPlayerTractorBeamImageView?.startAnimating()

        if let otherPlayerTractorBeamImageView =
        otherPlayerTractorBeamImageView {
            view.insertSubview(otherPlayerTractorBeamImageView,
            at: 4)
        }
    }
```

```
func endTractorFromNetwork() {
    otherPlayerTractorBeamImageView?.removeFromSuperview()
}
```

If you were to run the game now, you would see that when each user touches the screen, the tractor beam appears on both devices. We don't need to worry about locking the movement for the UFO while the tractor beam is on since this is handled for us in the single-player game, and movements are only transmitted to another device if they are acceptable on the single-player mode. Next, we need to add additional code to handle the hit test, so modify the hitTest function, as follows:

```
func hitTest() -> UIImageView? {
    if !tractorBeamOn {
        return nil
    }

    for x in 0..<(cowArray?.count ?? 0) {
        let tempCow = cowArray?[x] as? UIImageView
        let cowLayer = tempCow?.layer.presentation()
        let cowFrame = cowLayer?.frame

        if cowFrame?.intersects(tractorBeamImageView?.frame
        ?? CGRect.zero) ?? false {
            tempCow?.frame = cowLayer?.frame ?? CGRect.zero
            tempCow?.layer.removeAllAnimations()

            if gameIsMultiplayer {
                gcManager?.sendStringToAllPeers(String(for
                mat: "$abductCowAtIndex:%i", x), reliable:
                true)
            }
```

```
        return tempCow
    }
  }

  return nil
  }
}
```

Here we are using the same trick that we used earlier when we populated the cow array. Because we sent the data reliably to enter objects into our array, we know that the order of the array is always going to be the same. Because we know the order of the array, we can pass the index of the cow we want to modify. In addition to sending the data, we also need to write a new if statement to catch this message, as shown in the following. You can see this method is set up a lot like the score method in which we extract the value that we are interested in and call a new method using it:

```
else if dataDictionary["data"]?.hasPrefix("$abductCowAtIndex:")
?? false {
        let index = Int(dataDictionary["data"]?.
        replacingOccurrences(of: "$abductCowAtIndex:",
        with: "") ?? "") ?? 0
        abductCowFromNetwork(at: index)
}
```

The following two functions handle the abduction animations that are received over the network. They are both very similar to the functions that we use to animate an abduction in the single-player mode. You could even modify your existing functions to handle the network behavior by calling them with a flag to indicate that they are coming from a remote device.

```
func abductCowFromNetwork(at x: Int) {
        otherPlayerCurrentAbductee = cowArray?[x] as?
        UIImageView
```

```
        //otherPlayerCurrentAbductee?.frame =
        otherPlayerCurrentAbductee?.frame    // Skipping
        redundant initializing to itself
        otherPlayerCurrentAbductee?.layer.removeAllAnimations()

        UIView.animate(
            withDuration: 4.0,
            delay: 0,
            options: [.curveEaseIn, .beginFromCurrentState],
            animations: {
                var frame = self.otherPlayerCurrentAbductee?.
                frame
                frame?.origin.y = self.otherPlayerImageView?.
                frame.origin.y ?? 0.0
                self.otherPlayerCurrentAbductee?.frame = frame
                ?? CGRect.zero
            },
            completion: finishAbductingFromNetwork
        )
    }

func finishAbductingFromNetwork(_ finished: Bool) {
        cowArray = cowArray?.filter({ ($0) as AnyObject !==
        (otherPlayerCurrentAbductee) as AnyObject })
        endTractorFromNetwork()

        otherPlayerCurrentAbductee?.layer.removeAllAnimations()
        otherPlayerCurrentAbductee?.removeFromSuperview()

        otherPlayerCurrentAbductee = nil
```

```
if isHost {
    spawnCow()
}
}
```

We also need to do some overhead to make sure we don't create any new bugs. For example, we add a new pointer to keep track of which cow the enemy is currently abducting, if any. If you recall, in the updateCowPaths method, we don't want to update the path for the cow that is being abducted because it will break the animation that is being used for the abduction. We need to modify that method to also ignore whatever cow the enemy happens to be abducting. If you were to run the game again, you would now notice that we have a fully functional multiplayer game, as seen in Figure 7-4.

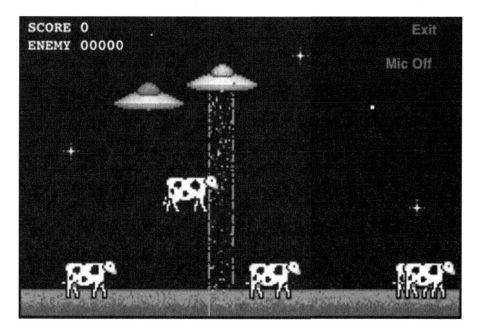

Figure 7-4. *A fully functional multiplayer UFO game being played by two people using a Bluetooth connection*

Disconnections

The last step that we need to take when working with multiplayer support is to add in logic to handle disconnections and other failures that are unrecoverable. Luckily for us, Apple's APIs handle most of the legwork. We do, however, want to add a more universal call to our GameCenterManager class to make things easier for us.

```swift
func disconnect() {
    switch matchOrSession {
    case .match(let match):
        match.disconnect()
    case .session(let session):
        session.disconnect()
    case .none:
        break
    }
}
```

This method should be called whenever you wish to end a multiplayer game. It will make sure that the peers are safely disconnected and prevent a number of issues that would be very hard to troubleshoot.

Summary

In this chapter, we covered a lot of information in a very condensed manner. You learned how to send and receive data between two or more iOS, Mac, or Apple TV devices using Game Center networking. In addition, you learned how to handle network state changes, such as disconnections. We put the principles learned in this chapter into use in our UFO game, creating a multiplayer iOS game from the ground up in less than seven chapters. In the next chapter, we will explore Game Center's turn-based gaming APIs, which function differently enough from real-time gaming to warrant a completely new sample project and game.

CHAPTER 8

Turn-Based Gaming with Game Center

Slightly after the initial release of Game Center, Apple would later update the framework with turn-based gaming support, in addition to the real-time gaming functionality you are familiar with from the previous chapters of this book. With turn-based gaming, you can now provide your users with asynchronous gaming. Turn-based games are simply any game in which players take turns playing, with notable examples such as in tic-tac-toe, chess, Battleship, and Dungeons & Dragons.

Turn-based gaming on iOS, Mac, and Apple TV has become very popular in the past several years, arguably starting with the megahit Words with Friends. Words with Friends, shown in Figure 8-1, is an asynchronous word game similar to Scrabble. Each player receives a selection of letters that they must play, in turn, on a board to create a word. There are points awarded based on the difficulty of the word, as well as layout on the board. Turn-based gaming is traditionally done with a store and forward network–type platform; the server holds on to the game data until the next client logs in and retrieves it. Asynchronous games have traditionally been more casual games and don't require all players to be present at all times, although some games do require immediate response and playing.

© Kyle Richter and Beau G. Bolle 2022
K. Richter and B. G. Bolle, *Beginning iOS Game Center and GameKit*,
https://doi.org/10.1007/978-1-4842-7756-0_8

Figure 8-1. *Words with Friends by Zynga*

Before the introduction of turn-based gaming, Game Center had provided real-time gaming in which all the devices involved needed to be active and logged in continuously throughout the multiplayer experience. Turn-based gaming adds a more casual experience, letting people run up to 20 matches at a time and only playing when it is their turn in a particular match.

Prior to these enhancements, writing this type of game would have required you to write and deploy your own server to handle the game interaction. Now, you can add the networking component of turn-based gaming and be up and running in less than a day of work. In this chapter, we explore how to write a simple tic-tac-toe game using Game Center's turn-based gaming APIs.

A New Sample Project

Unfortunately, our existing UFOs sample game is not a suitable experience for testing turn-based gaming. It wouldn't make much sense to have each player make a move and then wait for the other player to catch up. Luckily, there is another very simple type of game that we can build a project around: tic-tac-toe. This classic children's game is something almost all of us have played and we have experience with the rules and strategy.

We begin by creating a new storyboard-based iOS App project. There are three views that we will be working with throughout the project:

- Main View: This view simply contains a button that launches the HomeViewController, which we'll create in the following.

- GKTurnBasedMatchmakerViewController: This is the view provided by Apple to create and resume turn-based games. You will not need to create this view yourself.

- GameViewController: This is the class that handles user input, determining winners and ties, and populating the game board at the start of each turn.

We begin by working with the home view. These files will be created for you when you create the new project. The very first thing we need to do is make sure to import the proper GameKit frameworks and add our reusable GameCenterManager class that we have been working on throughout this book; you can include the existing one from Chapter 8. We also need to create a single button in the view to start a new game, as shown in Figure 8-2.

Figure 8-2. *The main view for our new tic-tac-toe game*

The file for the new home view controller class should match the following code snippet. We need to adhere to the GameCenterManagerDelegate as well as the GKTurnBasedMatchmakerViewController. As in the previous chapters, we also need to create a class instance of GameCenterManager. The last thing that needs to be added is an IBAction to begin a new game. Make sure to hook up the Start New Game button to the IBAction in the storyboard.

We also need to modify the viewDidLoad function to check for and then authenticate our local user with Game Center. This is the same approach that we followed in Chapter 2.

```
class HomeViewController: UIViewController {

    var gcManager: GameCenterManager?

    override func viewDidLoad() {
        super.viewDidLoad()

        NotificationCenter.default.addObserver(
            self,
            selector: #selector(localUserAuthentication
            Changed(_:)),
            name: .GKPlayerAuthenticationDidChange
            NotificationName,
            object: nil)

        gcManager = GameCenterManager()
        gcManager?.authenticateLocalUser(self)
    }

}
```

We also need to implement one delegate function to monitor for successful authentication and local user changes. We are using this function to print some debugging output.

```
@objc func localUserAuthenticationChanged(_ notification:
Notification?) {
    if let object = notification?.object {
        print("Authentication Changed: \(object)")
    }
}
```

In the next section, we will see how to call the GKTurnBasedMatchmakerViewController and how to handle the delegate functions that are required in order to handle errors and resume or create new matches.

GKTurnBasedMatchmakerViewController

Apple provides a default class to present the GUI for creating a new turn-based match. For programmatically creating a match, see the later section "Programmatic Matches."

We begin by working with a new matchmaker object in the IBAction for the single button that we created in the previous section. The approach that we use here is very similar to Game Center matchmaking. Take a look at the following sample code. This function is very similar to the previous examples of working with real-time gaming and matchmaking, with the notable change being switching to GKTurnBasedMatchmakerViewController and turnBasedMatchmakerDelegate instead of their real-time peers. The user will be presented with a view similar to the one shown in Figure 8-3.

```
@IBAction func showMatchmaker() {
    let match = GKMatchRequest()
    match.minPlayers = 2
    match.maxPlayers = 2

    let turnMatchmakerVC = GKTurnBasedMatchmakerViewController(
    matchRequest: match)

    turnMatchmakerVC.turnBasedMatchmakerDelegate = self

    present(turnMatchmakerVC, animated: true)
}
```

Note   As with all Game Center functionality, you must first authenticate with Game Center before you can create a new turn-based game match.

There are four delegate functions that you need to implement to conform to the GKTurnBasedMatchmakerViewControllerDelegate. The first handles the user canceling in the matchmaker. The only requirement here is to call dismiss on the game picker modal. You may add additional logic, as required, for your app.

```
extension HomeViewController:
GKTurnBasedMatchmakerViewControllerDelegate {

    func turnBasedMatchmakerViewControllerWasCancelled(_
    viewController: GKTurnBasedMatchmakerViewController) {
        dismiss(animated: true)
    }

}
```

Important   The list of current games does not update until you close and reopen the GKTurnBasedMatchmakerViewController.

Figure 8-3. *Starting a new turn-based match*

We also need to implement a delegate function to catch any errors that occur during this phase. The following function is called whenever an error is encountered during the matchmaking process. For debugging purposes, we are printing the error to the console; however, you will want to inform the user that an error has occurred.

```
func turnBasedMatchmakerViewController(_ viewController:
GKTurnBasedMatchmakerViewController, didFailWithError error:
Error) {
    print("Turn Based Matchmaker Failed with Error:
    \(error.localizedDescription)")
}
```

The last delegate function that we discuss in this section handles the user quitting a match from the matchmaker screen. This is accomplished by swiping from right to left across a game and selecting the quit option. We pass in logic that the quitting player will be the losing player of the match and that the remote player will be marked the winner. If you do not call the proper function here, you will be able to quit a game, but it will reappear within a few seconds.

```
func turnBasedMatchmakerViewController(_ viewController:
GKTurnBasedMatchmakerViewController, playerQuitFor match:
GKTurnBasedMatch) {
        guard let localParticipant = match.participants.
        first(where: { $0.player == GKLocalPlayer.local }),
            let otherParticipant = match.participants.
            first(where: {$0 != localParticipant}) else {
          return
        }
        localParticipant.matchOutcome = .quit
        otherParticipant.matchOutcome = .won

        match.endMatchInTurn(withMatch: match.matchData ??
        Data()) { error in
```

```
    if let error = error {
        print("An error occurred ending match: \(error.
        localizedDescription)")
    }
  }
}
```

The final required function, didFindMatch, is discussed in the next section, "Starting a New Game."

Establishing Game State

Before we can really dive into the new game, it is important for us to do some foundation laying in order to make life easier down the road. The first thing we will do is set up the possible states of the game. Tic-tac-toe is a very simple game, but there can still be several active states; the first two will be applicable to any turn-based game and covering which player we are currently waiting on to make their move. The following three states cover a game ending status from local player winning, remote player winning, or a tied match:

```
private enum GameStatus {
    case waitingForLocalPlayer
    case waitingForOtherPlayer
    case localPlayerWon
    case otherPlayerWon
    case playersTied
}
```

The next piece of groundwork that needs to be laid will enable the functionality to detect the current state of the game. We will need to determine what the winning combinations of gameplay are to detect if they have occurred throughout the gameplay. We are using a brute force approach to see if we have a winner, by checking all the rows and columns for three matching players. We also need to check for a tie if there are no more places to move.

```
private var currentGameStatus: GameStatus {
    if let localParticipant = localParticipant {
        switch localParticipant.matchOutcome {
        case .none:
            break
        case .quit, .lost, .timeExpired:
            return .otherPlayerWon
        case .won, .first, .second, .third, .fourth,
        .customRange:
            return .localPlayerWon
        case .tied:
            return .playersTied
        @unknown default:
            print("Unknown GKTurnBasedParticipant.matchOutcome
            received. Assuming game is in progress.")
        }
    }

    let winningCombinations = [
        // horizontal
        [0, 1, 2],
        [3, 4, 5],
        [6, 7, 8],
```

```
    // vertical
        [0, 3, 6],
        [1, 4, 7],
        [2, 5, 8],

        // diagonal
        [0, 4, 8],
        [2, 4, 6],
    ]

    let winningCombination = winningCombinations.first
     { combo in
        let filledSquares: [Player] = combo.compactMap{
        gameBoard[$0] }.filter{ $0 != .none}
        guard filledSquares.count == combo.count else { return
        false }
        let uniquePlayers = Set(filledSquares)
        return uniquePlayers.count == 1
    }
    guard let winningPlayerIndex = winningCombination?[0], let
    winningPlayer = gameBoard[winningPlayerIndex] else {
        guard gameBoard.count != 9 else { return .playersTied }

        return localPlayerIsCurrentParticipant ?
        .waitingForLocalPlayer : .waitingForOtherPlayer
    }
    return winningPlayer == localPlayer ? .localPlayerWon :
    .otherPlayerWon
}
```

Finally, we need to set up some functions to encode and store the state of the game board. This is done by simply storing the button labels into a JSONEncoder. This allows for easy and safe storage of information as well as easy network transmittal if our game required it.

```
private typealias GameBoard = [Int: Player]
    private var gameBoard: GameBoard = [:] {
        didSet {
            logGameBoard("didSet")
        }
    }
    private var gameBoardData: Data? {
        logGameBoard("Serializing")
        return try? JSONEncoder().encode(gameBoard)
    }

    private func logGameBoard(_ label: String) {
        print((["\(label):"] + gameBoard.map{ "\($0.key): \($0.
        value.buttonTitle ?? "")" }).joined(separator: "\n"))
    }
    private var logError: (Error?) -> Void = { error in
        guard let error = error else { return }
        print("An error occurred updating turn: \(error.
         localizedDescription)")
    }
```

Starting a New Game

Starting a new match with turn-based gaming is a very straightforward and simple process. To do so, you need to implement the following function as part of the delegate. This new function dismisses the GKTurnBasedMatchmakerViewController and then passes a copy of the match object to your Game Controller. The following code snippet is the procedure we follow for tic-tac-toe:

```
func turnBasedMatchmakerViewController(_ viewController:
GKTurnBasedMatchmakerViewController, didFind match:
GKTurnBasedMatch) {
    performSegue(withIdentifier: "PlayGame", sender: match)
    dismiss(animated: true)
}
```

Then we pass the match to the destination when the segue is prepared.

```
override func prepare(for segue: UIStoryboardSegue,
sender: Any?) {
    guard
        segue.identifier == "PlayGame",
        let match = sender as? GKTurnBasedMatch,
        let game = segue.destination as? GameViewController
    else { return }

    game.match = match
}
```

Let's now switch attention to the GameViewController class.

Important   You are strictly limited to passing only 4k of data with each new turn. If you cannot limit your game data to less than 4k, you can use a URL to point to a server holding the complete data set. Alternatively, you could pass only the delta of the game state and store the existing data locally.

```swift
class GameViewController: UIViewController {

    var match: GKTurnBasedMatch? {
        didSet {
            loadMatchData()
        }
    }

    @IBOutlet private var buttons: [UIButton]!
    @IBOutlet private var teamLabel: UILabel!
    @IBOutlet private var statusLabel: UILabel!
    @IBOutlet private var forfeitButton: UIButton!

    @IBAction private func makeMove(_ sender: UIButton) {
    }
    @IBAction func forfeitTapped() {
    }

}
```

We first need to configure the actual game view (GameViewController).
We need nine spots for the user to move in the tic-tac-toe game, as well as
a forfeit option and a pair of labels to inform players whose turn it is.

We use simple UIButtons to handle user input. Modify the storyboard
with a layout similar to that pictured in Figure 8-4. You need to create
IBOutlets for each of the buttons and the label as well as new IBAction
functions for both making a move and forfeiting. Connect all the board
buttons to the makeMove function that you previously created. We also
need to set tags on the UIButtons to help us locate them. Begin with tag
1 in the upper-left corner and move left to right, up to down, numbering
them.

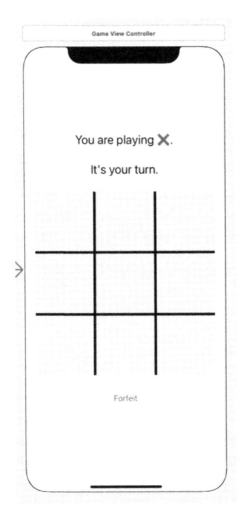

Figure 8-4. *A view of the game board, as seen from the storyboard editor*

You now have two new functions in your game view controller, as well as nine button outlets and one label outlet. This covers how to begin a new turn-based gaming match. In the next section, we look at how to make a move and pass control to the next player.

Making the First Move

The first thing we need to do in a new match-based game, before we make a move, is determine who the player is representing. In our example game, there are two sides: X and O. We are going to set the first person to always be X and the second to always be O. This means that X will always make the first move. With this setup, it becomes easy to determine who the player currently is representing using the following code and convenience functions.

The first four pieces of code declare private variables to make determining the local player, the remote player, the current player, and the next player easier to retrieve. After that a new struct is created for the player which will allow us to easily store state information on the progress of the game. Finally, some additional variables are set up to easily work with current player and the next player.

```swift
private var localParticipant: GKTurnBasedParticipant? {
    match?.participants.first{ $0.player == GKLocalPlayer.
    local }
}
private var otherParticipant: GKTurnBasedParticipant? {
    guard let localParticipant = localParticipant else {
    return nil }

    return match?.participants.first{ $0 != localParticipant }
}
private var localPlayerIsCurrentParticipant: Bool {
    guard let localParticipant = localParticipant else { return
    false }

    return match?.currentParticipant == localParticipant
}
```

```swift
private var nextParticipant: GKTurnBasedParticipant? {
    guard let localParticipant = localParticipant else { return
    nil }

    return localPlayerIsCurrentParticipant ? otherParticipant :
    localParticipant
}

private enum Player: String, Codable {
    case none
    case x
    case o

    var title: String {
        switch self {
        case .none: return "unknown"
        case .x: return "✕"
        case .o: return "◯"
        }
    }
    var buttonTitle: String? {
        switch self {
        case .none: return nil
        case .x, .o: return title
        }
    }
}
private var localPlayer: Player = .none
private var otherPlayer: Player {
    switch localPlayer {
    case .none: return .none
    case .x: return .o
```

```swift
        case .o: return .x
        }
}
private var currentPlayer: Player {
    if let currentParticipant = match?.currentParticipant, let
    firstParticipant = match?.participants.first {
        return currentParticipant == firstParticipant ?
        .x : .o
    }
    return .none
}
private var nextPlayer: Player {
    switch currentPlayer {
    case .x: return .o
    case .o, .none: return .x
    }
}
```

After we have determined who the users are, then we can allow them to make a move. We will modify the code for the action to which the nine game buttons are connected. First, let's take a look at the function that will be called when a play space button is tapped.

```swift
@IBAction private func makeMove(_ sender: UIButton) {
    guard let index = buttons.firstIndex(of: sender) else {
    return }

    gameBoard[index] = localPlayer
    sendMatchData()
}
```

Next, the sendMatchData function is called, in which the current game state is determined to either be the local player has finished their move to end the turn, the local player has won so end the match, the players have tied so end the match, or the remote player is currently being waited on.

```
private func sendMatchData() {
    switch currentGameStatus {
    case .waitingForLocalPlayer:
        endTurn()
    case .localPlayerWon:
        endMatchInTurn(participantOutcome: .won,
        nextParticipantOutcome: .lost)
    case .playersTied:
        endMatchInTurn(participantOutcome: .tied,
        nextParticipantOutcome: .tied)
    case .waitingForOtherPlayer, .otherPlayerWon:
        break
    }
}
```

If the game state determined that it is the next player's turn, then endTurn is called. Once the proper variables have been set for the match, the next player and the current board data match.endTurn are then called and the view is updated. This will let Game Center know it is the remote player's turn.

```
private func endTurn() {
    guard let match = match, let nextParticipant =
    nextParticipant, let gameBoardData = gameBoardData else {
    return }

    match.endTurn(withNextParticipants: [nextParticipant],
    turnTimeout: GKTurnTimeoutDefault, match: gameBoardData) {
    [weak self] error in
```

```
        self?.logError(error)
        self?.updateView()
    }
}
```

In the event that the game is finished in a tie or a win, then endMatchInTurn is called. participantOutcome out is passed into the function with either win or tie depending on the game state. There are other options available for this variable such as quit, lost, timeExpired, and custom values, which are not used in our simple tic-tac-toe example but may be applicable to your game.

```
private func endMatchInTurn(participantOutcome:
GKTurnBasedMatch.Outcome, nextParticipantOutcome:
GKTurnBasedMatch.Outcome?) {
        guard let match = match,
            let currentParticipant = match.
            currentParticipant,
            let nextParticipant = nextParticipant,
            let gameBoardData = gameBoardData else { return }

        currentParticipant.matchOutcome = participantOutcome
        if let nextParticipantOutcome = nextParticipantOutcome {
            nextParticipant.matchOutcome =
            nextParticipantOutcome
        }
        match.endMatchInTurn(withMatch: gameBoardData)
        { [weak self] error in
            self?.logError(error)
            self?.loadMatchData()
        }
    }
```

Note   The size and order of the participant's array are determined when the match first begins and will be the same throughout the match and on each device.

Tip   You might see that there are nil objects in the participant array; these are placeholders for unmatched players. Game Center will only match new players when it is their turn to move. This means that every time you are auto-matched, it will be your turn to move.

The last thing that we will do at the end of each move is send the new game data to the next player. This player will, in turn, update the game state and send it to the next player (which happens to be the first player again).

GKLocalPlayerListener Extensions

We will be adding two extension functions GKLocalPlayerListener in order to monitor for changes in turn events as well as the end of a match. These will also allow us to update the match data as the game progresses.

```
extension GameViewController: GKLocalPlayerListener {
    func player(_ player: GKPlayer, receivedTurnEventFor match:
    GKTurnBasedMatch, didBecomeActive: Bool) {
        guard match.matchID == self.match?.matchID else {
        return }
        self.match = match
    }
}
```

```
func player(_ player: GKPlayer, matchEnded match:
GKTurnBasedMatch) {
    guard match.matchID == self.match?.matchID else {
    return }
    self.match = match
}

}
```

Continuing a Game in Progress

When you resume a game on your next turn, assuming it is not the first turn of a match, you will need to first restore the game state to its current position. To do this, we begin by modifying our viewDidLoad function to get the current match data. We in turn call an updateView function to set up the current game board. The first step of this process is determining the current game state. Among other things, here we can determine if the game is ended and, if not, whose turn it currently is. We also parse the gameboard data and fill in the current Xs and Os to match the game history.

```
override func viewDidLoad() {
    super.viewDidLoad()

    GKLocalPlayer.local.register(self)
    updateView()
}

private func updateView() {
    teamLabel.text = "You are playing \(localPlayer.title)."

    let statusText: String
    let forfeitButtonEnabled: Bool
```

```swift
        switch currentGameStatus {
        case .waitingForLocalPlayer:
            statusText = "It's your turn."
            forfeitButtonEnabled = true
        case .waitingForOtherPlayer:
            statusText = "It's \(otherPlayer.title)'s turn."
            forfeitButtonEnabled = true
        case .localPlayerWon:
            statusText = "You won!"
            forfeitButtonEnabled = false
        case .otherPlayerWon:
            statusText = "You lost."
            forfeitButtonEnabled = false
        case .playersTied:
            statusText = "It's a tie."
            forfeitButtonEnabled = false
        }
        statusLabel.text = statusText
        forfeitButton.isEnabled = forfeitButtonEnabled

        for index in 0..<9 {
            let player = gameBoard[index] ?? .none
            let button = buttons[index]
            button.setTitle(player.buttonTitle, for: .normal)
            button.isEnabled = localPlayerIsCurrentParticipant
            && player == .none
        }
    }

private func loadMatchData() {
        guard let match = match, let firstMatchParticipant =
        match.participants.first else {
            localPlayer = .none
```

```swift
        gameBoard = GameBoard()
        updateView()
        return
    }

    localPlayer = firstMatchParticipant.player ==
    GKLocalPlayer.local ? .x : .o
    match.loadMatchData { (data, error) in
        if let error = error {
            print("Load Match Data: \(error.
            localizedDescription)")
            return
        }
        if self.otherParticipant?.matchOutcome == .quit,
        self.localParticipant?.matchOutcome != .won {
            self.endMatchInTurn(participantOutcome: .won,
            nextParticipantOutcome: nil)
            return
        }
        guard let data = data else { return }

        do {
            self.gameBoard = try JSONDecoder().
            decode(GameBoard.self, from: data)
        } catch {
            self.gameBoard = GameBoard()
        }
        self.updateView()
    }
}
```

> **Tip**   If you persist the game state locally, you will only need to
> update the turns that have occurred since your last move. This
> approach will help you keep packet sizes under the 4k limit.

With the code in place, you can now play through a complete round of
tic-tac-toe using two Game Center accounts; however, the game will never
detect a winner or a draw. In the next section, we look at the logic required
to detect an end-of-game event.

Quitting and Forfeiting

A player can quit a match at any time by swiping across it from the
matchmaker view controller. However, you might want to add a path for
your users to forfeit or quit a match from inside of your game itself. To
allow a player to forfeit a match, use the following code snippet. This will
allow a player to quit a game even if it is not currently their turn:

```
@IBAction func forfeitTapped() {
    if localPlayerIsCurrentParticipant {
        endMatchInTurn(participantOutcome: .quit,
        nextParticipantOutcome: .won)
    } else {
        quitMatchOutOfTurn()
    }
}
}

    private func quitMatchOutOfTurn() {
        guard let match = match else { return }
```

```
    match.participantQuitOutOfTurn(with: .quit) { [weak
    self] error in
        self?.logError(error)
        self?.loadMatchData()
    }
}
```

Programmatic Matches

If you want to bypass the GKTurnBasedMatchmakerViewController and implement your own GUI, there is an option to do so. Using the following function will create a new match without having the user go through the matchmaker:

```
func findMatch() {
    let match = GKMatchRequest()

    match.minPlayers = 2
    match.maxPlayers = 2

    GKTurnBasedMatch.find(for: match) { match, error in
        if let error = error {
            print("An error occurred when finding a match:
            \(error.localizedDescription)")
            return
        }

        // Start new game with returned match.
    }
}
```

In addition to creating a game, you need to be able to load a list of existing games for your local user. You can do so with the following function:

```
func loadMatches() {
    GKTurnBasedMatch.loadMatches { matches, error in
        if let error = error {
            print("An error occurred while loading matches:
            \(error.localizedDescription)")
            return
        }

        print("Existing Matches: \(matches ?? [])")
    }
}
```

Note   Because both of these functions use background tasks in order to handle the request, the code that you implement within the block needs to be thread safe.

GKTurnBasedEventHandler

The GKTurnBasedEventHandler is a delegate protocol that is responsible for handling important messages related to turn-based games. To set a delegate for events, use the following code:

```
[[GKTurnBasedEventHandler sharedTurnBasedEventHandler]
setDelegate: self];
```

The protocol has three optional functions.

- handleInviteFromGameCenter: When your delegate receives this function, it should populate a new GKMatchRequest with the playersToInvite that are passed in through the function. You then need to begin a new match or present the matchmaker GUI. This function is called when the user accepts a match invite from a friend.

- handleTurnEventForMatch: Your delegate receives this message when the user has accepted a push notification for an in-progress match. You need to end whatever task you are performing and display the game for the match that is passed in with this function.

- handleMatchEnded: When your delegate receives this message, it should display the match's results and game-over views to the player and allow the player the option of removing the match data from Game Center.

Summary

In this chapter, we learned about the new turn-based gaming in Game Center. We worked with our existing GameCenterManager class and wrote an entirely new sample game to work with the turn-based technology. You should now have a firm grasp on how to create a new turn-based game, as well as retain and send turn data between peers. With the skills learned in this chapter, you should now be able to easily get the networking component of turn-based gaming up and running in a few hours.

In the next chapter, we will be looking at another exciting topic: voice chat. Apple has gone through tremendous lengths to make voice-over IP easy to use in iOS, Mac, and Apple TV apps, and we will explore how to quickly get VOIP up and running in your Game Center– or GameKit–enabled apps.

CHAPTER 9

Voice Chat

Voice chat, more than any other service provided as part of Game Center, is a true testament to Apple engineering. Apple has turned one of the most complicated features on other platforms into one of the easiest to implement on iOS, Mac, and Apple TV devices. When working with Voice over Internet Protocol (VOIP) on other platforms, it is often the most complex and daunting task of an entire project. In this chapter, we will explore how to add voice chat services to UFOs or any Apple platform app. The shortness of this chapter is evidence of how much work Apple has put into this technology to bring it within the grasp of even the greenest of developers.

Note In this chapter, we return to the UFOs project. We're done with tic-tac-toe.

Voice Chat for Game Center

We begin by looking at voice chat for Game Center. Using a GKMatch to create a voice chat session has many advantages, such as ease of use, quickness to implement, and reduced required overhead compared to using GameKit or having to implement your own system. A GKMatch voice chat can have multiple channels, each with an associated list of recipients. For example, you could have one channel for teammates in a first-person

© Kyle Richter and Beau G. Bolle 2022
K. Richter and B. G. Bolle, *Beginning iOS Game Center and GameKit*,
https://doi.org/10.1007/978-1-4842-7756-0_9

shooter game and another channel for all players. This would allow you to talk about tactics for winning the match without giving away information to the other teams.

Note   Voice chat using a GKMatch is only available to participants who are connected to the Internet via Wi-Fi; voice chat does not support cellular networks.

Creating an Audio Session

Before you can begin to work with voice chat, you first need to create a new audio session. It is important to do this before you begin any chat services. If you create the audio session after you create the chat session, you will not be able to send or receive voice data. In the following example, we create a new audio session that allows our app to play and record audio and then set it to Active.

Tip   Your app might already use an audio session for playing sound effects; if you have already created an audio session, you are not required to make a new one. If you are reusing an existing audio session, make sure that you set it to allow both play and record functionality.

```
var error: Error? = nil

let audioSession = AVAudioSession.sharedInstance()
do {
    try audioSession.setCategory(.playAndRecord)
} catch (let err){
    error = err
}
```

```
do {
    try audioSession.setActive(true)
} catch (let err) {
    error = err
}

if let error = error {
    print("An error occurred while starting audio session:
    \(error.localizedDescription)")
}
```

Creating New Voice Channels

You can have as many voice chat channels as you want in your app, and each peer can register to be part of as many channels as they want. Channels are created and organized by a name string. This is how we will determine what channels we want the user to join. When two or more peers join a channel with the same name, they are connected to the same chat.

The code snippet that follows shows an example of how to create three different channels. Take note that the channels are created with the GKMatch object that is returned to us when we begin a new Game Center-based networking game:

```
let allChannel = match.voiceChat(withName: "allPlayers")
let teamChannel = match.voiceChat(withName: "blueTeam")
let squadChannel = match.voiceChat(withName: "BlueTeamSquad2")
```

In this example, we have a channel for communicating with all players, a channel for communicating with our entire team, and a third channel that is used to talk with our squad. Just because channels have been created doesn't mean that they are automatically turned on. In the next section, we will look at how to start and stop communication on a specific channel.

Starting and Stopping Voice Chat

In the previous section, we created three new voice channels for use with Game Center-type voice chat. When you want to transmit and receive voice on those channels, you need to first tell the API that you want to begin using that channel. After you are connected to a channel, you are able to send and receive data from that channel. If you want to connect to a channel and do not want to transmit any voice audio, see the following section on muting the microphone.

To begin using a voice channel, you need to call the start method on the GKVoiceChat object that was created in the previous section.

```
allChannel?.start()
teamChannel?.start()
```

When you want to leave a channel, you simply call the stop method. This is a better approach than simply muting all participants in the channel because the app will not be required to receive additional network data. A stopped channel can be restarted at any time.

```
allChannel?.stop()
teamChannel?.stop()
```

Tip   It is highly recommended that you provide both visual and audio indicators when you are transmitting voice data, such as a red light and a click sound. This reduces the chance that a user will accidentally transmit voice data when they don't intend to. Always remember that a user's microphone and transmitted voice should be treated as sensitive data. As of iOS 14, there is a small indicator light in the notch area of the iPhone which indicates the microphone is currently live.

Chat Volume and Muting

The voice chat volume is set on a per-channel basis. Each channel has an associated property that can be used to lower the overall volume of that chat. You cannot raise the volume past what the user has selected as the device's current volume. To modify a channel's volume, add the following line of code:

```
allChannel?.volume = 0.5 //half of max volume
```

In addition, you can mute individual players in a channel by referencing their GKPlayer. Players can be muted and unmuted using the following two lines of code:

```
teamChannel?.setPlayer(player, muted: true)
teamChannel?.setPlayer(player, muted: false)
```

There might also be circumstances in which you do not want to transmit the user's voice at all times. By default, a user starts a chat in the muted state. You will need to unmute a user before he can begin to transmit voice data.

```
squadChannel?.isActive = true
```

Note   A user can only transmit voice on one channel at a time; if you unmute a channel, the API will automatically mute all other channels.

This is all that is required in order to completely enable voice chat in your Game Center–based networking app. Everything else, including sending and receiving the data, is handled for you by the APIs.

Monitoring Player State

I mentioned earlier in this chapter that it is important to let the user know that they are currently transmitting data. Letting the player see who is speaking is also an important step. By monitoring player state changes, you can determine which users are currently transmitting voice and highlight them in a player list or perform some other kind of indication of which player is speaking. The following block is easy to set up when you begin your chat and saves you from performing polling or delegate callbacks:

```
guard let allChannel = allChannel else {
    return
}

allChannel.playerVoiceChatStateDidChangeHandler = { player,
state in
    switch state {
    case .connected:
        print("Channel", allChannel.name, "connected.")
    case .disconnected:
        print("Channel", allChannel.name, "disconnected.")
    case .speaking:
        showSpeakingPlayer(player)
    case .silent:
        stopShowingSpeakingPlayer(player)
    case .connecting:
        print("Channel", allChannel.name, "is connecting.")
    @unknown default:
        print("Channel", allChannel.name, "received unknown
        state", state, ".")
    }
}
```

Note   Player state updates are handled per channel. You will need to configure one for each channel that you wish to watch for changes on.

Putting It Together

In this chapter, we modify our existing code base from Chapter 8. Begin there by creating a new audio session for your voice chat service. Add the following block of code to the UFOGameViewController.swift viewDidLoad() method. In addition, you need to add the AVFoundation. framework to your project. Modify the relevant section of the viewDidLoad method to match the following:

```
if gameIsMultiplayer == false {
        for _ in 0..<5 {
            spawnCow()
        }

        updateCowPaths()
    } else {

    generateAndSendHostNumber()

    var error: Error? = nil

    let audioSession = AVAudioSession.sharedInstance()
    do {
        try audioSession.setCategory(.playAndRecord)
    } catch (let err){
        error = err
    }
```

```
        do {
            try audioSession.setActive(true)
        } catch (let err) {
            error = err
        }

        if let error = error {
            print("An error occurred while starting audio
            session: \(error.localizedDescription)")
        }

        setupVoiceChat()
    }
```

Caution   Make sure the device you are building against has both a
speaker and a microphone available for use.

You also need to add a new method called setupVoiceChat. This
method will handle the basic configuration.

```
func setupVoiceChat() {
    mainChannel = peerMatch?.voiceChat(withName: "main")
    mainChannel?.start()
    mainChannel?.volume = 1.0
    mainChannel?.isActive = false
}
```

Hooking Up a User Interface

The last thing we need to do is hook up an action to turn our microphone on and off. I have decided to go with a simple toggle button for UFOs, but you may feel the need to implement a different approach. Add a new button, as shown in Figure 9-1, and hook up the new action posted next.

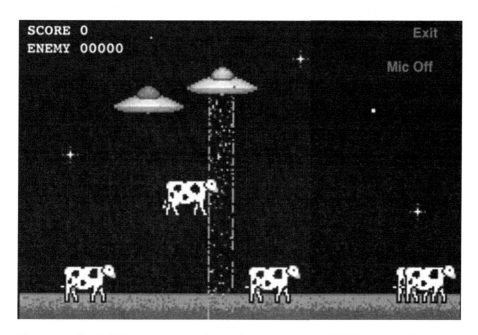

Figure 9-1. *Adding a microphone button to our UFO game demo*

```
@IBAction func startVoice(_ sender: Any) {
    micOn = !micOn

    if micOn {
        micButton.setTitle("Mic On", for: .normal)

        mainChannel?.isActive = true
```

```
    } else {
        micButton.setTitle("Mic Off", for: .normal)

        mainChannel?.isActive = false
    }
}
```

This method determines the current state of the microphone (on/off) and toggles it to the new state. When that happens, we update the button title and turn the microphone on or off for the type of network that we are using.

These are all the required steps to add voice chat into our UFO example project. If you run the game on two devices, you will be able to communicate with voice back and forth.

Summary

In this chapter, we learned how to incorporate a traditionally very complex technology into our iOS app with very little work. We explored the differences with using voice chat on both GameKit and Game Center, as well as implemented examples of both systems into our UFO demo game. You now have the skills required to add full-featured VOIP technology to any iPhone or iPad app. If you have been following the book along from the beginning, you now have all the skills needed to implement all aspects of GameKit and Game Center into your apps.

In the next chapter, we will take a look at another important technology when writing games or apps for iOS—StoreKit. Using StoreKit technology, we will learn how to sell additional features and add-ons to your product.

CHAPTER 10

In-App Purchase with StoreKit

Throughout this book, we have been working with both Game Center and GameKit to add rich social networking into your iOS, Mac, and Apple TV apps. However, there is another important feature quickly becoming popular in modern software: in-app purchases. Allowing your users to purchase upgrades or additional content for your app, from directly within your app, opens up a potentially significant new revenue stream. Over the past decade, a new business model has emerged called Freemium. Freemium is a type of game or product that is offered to your users for free but is monetized through selling add-ons.

We will be taking a look at We Rule by ngmoco:) as an example. The game is initially offered for free for both iPhone and iPad players. Each user is in control of a virtual kingdom, in which they are responsible for constructing buildings and growing crops. The user generates "mojo" over time and can use that in-app currency to create new structures and farms. However, some users want to construct faster than is normally allowed due the restrictive nature of mojo, which slowly accumulates. These power-users can visit the in-app store to purchase more mojo in bulk. It offers a number of purchases ranging from very affordable to shockingly expensive. It is important to cater to both types of users when working with sellable add-ons. Some of your users will be interested in spending one

© Kyle Richter and Beau G. Bolle 2022
K. Richter and B. G. Bolle, *Beginning iOS Game Center and GameKit*,
https://doi.org/10.1007/978-1-4842-7756-0_10

or two dollars occasionally, while some will be power-users who want to spend one hundred dollars, or more, at a time.

Freemium has become such a strong business model that ngmoco:) has stopped working on games that do not fit into the Freemium model, going so far as to even cancel Rolando 3 in mid-development because it couldn't be adapted to the model. The model appears to be paying off well for ngmoco:). As shown in Figure 10-1, the current highest selling item in the We Rule store is a $9.99 item. This one in-app purchase is retailing for more than most stand-alone iOS games, and the reason it was able to get that customer is that it hooked them with a free game first.

In-App Purchases	
Pile of rubies	$9.99
Stack of rubies	$2.99
Starter pack	$0.99
Heap of rubies	$19.99
Mountain of rubies	$29.99
Super pack	$4.99
Rubies treasure	$99.99
Premium 3-day Trial	$4.99
Mega pack	$29.99
Monthly Premium	$14.99

Figure 10-1. *Current listing of the best-selling in-app purchases for We Rule by ngmoco:)*

Not all games or apps supported by in-app purchase need to be free. You can easily add additional features or unlocks in a paid game, such as the Mighty Eagle in Angry Birds. In-app purchase is also not only just for games. Almost any software can benefit from it, whether you are unlocking pro-level features or charging users a subscription for push notification support. As we dive into this chapter, we will explore how to add a full-featured in-app store to your iOS, Mac, and Apple TV software.

Setting Up Your App in App Store Connect

As with Game Center, we need to begin working with in-app purchases in App Store Connect:

1. Log in to App Store Connect (`https://appstoreconnect.apple.com/login`), as discussed in Chapter 2. You will need an existing project to work on. If you don't have a project created in App Store Connect yet, go ahead and create one.

2. Select the project you want to add in-app purchase support to. Then, click the button called Manage under In-App Purchases section.

Important   You have 90 days from creating an app to upload a binary for review. Make sure to save the in-app purchase configuration until you are within 90 days of finishing your project.

---

3. Selecting the Manage button will bring you to a screen for setting up a new product, as shown in Figure 10-2. Once there, click the plus (+) button.

In-App Purchases

 Your first in-app purchase must be submitted with a new app version. Create your in-app purchase, then select it from the app's In-App Purchases section under App Store and click Submit. Learn More

Once your binary has been uploaded and your first in-app purchase has been submitted for review, additional in-app purchases can be submitted using the table below.

In-App Purchases (0) ⊕   App-Specific Shared Secret

Click + to add an in-app purchase.

Figure 10-2. *Setting up your first in-app purchase in App Store Connect*

There are several types of in-app purchase products that you can configure. They are detailed here for your convenience:

- Consumable: A consumable in-app purchase must be purchased every time the user downloads it. These include in-game currency, as we saw in the We Rule example in the previous section. Figure 10-3 shows the consumable purchase setup screen.

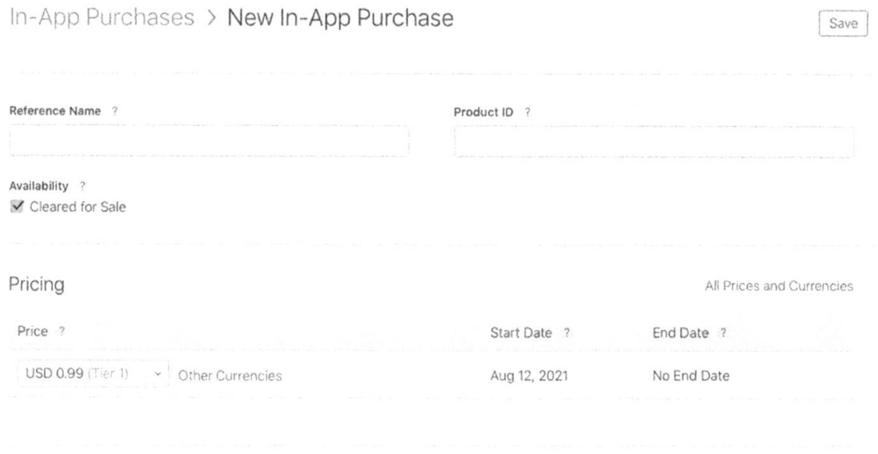

In-App Purchases > New In-App Purchase   [Save]

Reference Name   ?

Product ID   ?

Availability   ?
☑ Cleared for Sale

Pricing   All Prices and Currencies

Price   ?   Start Date   ?   End Date   ?

USD 0.99 (Tier 1)   ˅   Other Currencies   Aug 12, 2021   No End Date

Figure 10-3. *Setup screen for both consumable and non-consumable*
purchases in App Store Connect

- Non-Consumables: A non-consumable purchase
  needs to be purchased only once by each user and
  is often used for unlockable features. Examples of
  non-consumable purchases include additional levels,
  reusable power-ups, or additional content.

- Auto-Renewable Subscriptions: An auto-renewable
  subscription allows the user to purchase in-app content
  for a set duration of time. At the end of that time frame,
  the subscription will automatically renew and charge
  the customer unless they opt out. Magazines and
  newspapers follow this model, delivering a new issue
  every week or month until the user opts out. Figure 10-4
  shows the auto-renewable purchase setup screen.

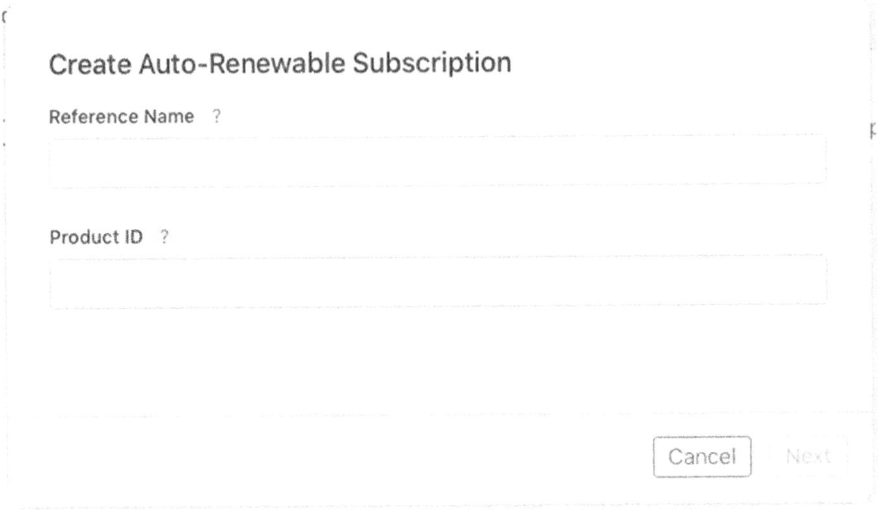

Create Auto-Renewable Subscription

Reference Name   ?

Product ID   ?

Cancel   Next

Figure 10-4. *Setup screen for auto-renewable purchases in App Store Connect*

- Non-Renewing Subscriptions: For the most part, renewable subscriptions have done away the need for this model. A non-renewing subscription functions the same as an auto-renewable subscription, except that a user is required to renew it every time it is set to expire.

Note   Auto-renewable subscriptions will be sent to all devices associated with the user's Apple ID.

We will begin by adding a non-consumable purchase. We will be using this item in our sample UFO game.

The first item we want to add is a paid upgrade to your current ship; name the item com.dragonforged.ufo.newShip1. I used the same title for both the product ID and the reference name. The reference name is for reference only when searching in App Store Connect, whereas the product ID is what will be used in your code base to identify this item.

After you have created a new item, you need to add at least one localized description and title, as shown in Figure 10-5. The last thing that you need to do is select a pricing tier for this item. You might have also noticed that there is a section for uploading a screenshot; we discuss this in the later section "Submitting a Purchase GUI Screenshot."

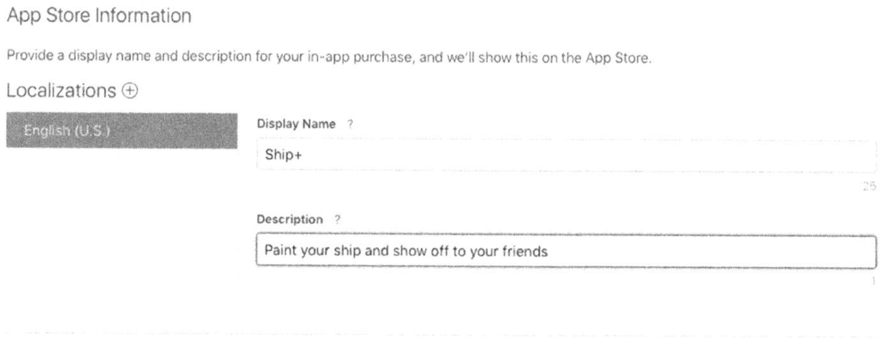

App Store Information

Provide a display name and description for your in-app purchase, and we'll show this on the App Store.

Localizations ⊕

English (U.S.)

Display Name   ?

Ship+

25

Description   ?

Paint your ship and show off to your friends

1

Figure 10-5. *Adding a localized description to a product in App Store Connect*

Adding a consumable product follows the same procedure as adding a non-consumable product. If you want to add a subscription-based product, there are a few new fields that you need to be aware of, as shown in Figure 10-6. When configuring a subscription, you need to define a duration. iTunes Connect allows you to set any of the following: one week, one month, two months, three months, six months, or one year. You also have the ability to offer a free subscription if the user agrees to a marketing campaign, such as providing you with their e-mail address.

(i) Before you can submit your in-app purchase for review, you must add at least one localization to your subscription group. Add localizations

Reference Name ?

com.dfsw.ufo.upgrade

Availability ?
✓ Cleared for Sale

Subscription Duration ?

1 Week   ⌄

Family Sharing ?
Allow family members to share this subscription without having to use each other's accounts.

Turn On

Apple ID ?
1580952544

Product ID ?
renewing

Group Reference Name ?
renewing

Figure 10-6. *Configuring subscription duration in iTunes Connect*

You should now have at least one product configured for in-app purchase. Your screen in App Store Connect should look similar to the one shown in Figure 10-7. This concludes the initial configuration that we need to do in App Store Connect to get in-app purchases working. In the next section, we begin to work with the code required to complete a purchase on a device.

Note   Don't worry about the "Missing Metadata" error yet; this will be handled later in the process. You will still be able to test your purchases while waiting to upload a screenshot.

In-App Purchases (2) ⊕   Q Search   App-Specific Shared Secret

Reference Name ^	Type	Product ID	Status
com.dfsw.ufo.newship	Consumable	Newship	Missing Metadata
com.dfsw.ufo.upgrade	Auto-Renewable Subscription	renewing	Missing Metadata

Figure 10-7. *Products set up and ready for use in our app*

Adding Products to Your App

Unlike with Game Center, Apple does not offer a predesigned GUI for in-app purchases. You, as the developer, are required to design a storefront for your user. In this section, we learn how to get products that you add in iTunes Connect to show up for sale in your app.

Note   It can take several hours for new purchases and changes to be reflected. If you double-check everything and are still not seeing products, wait a few hours and try again.

App IDs and In-App Purchase

When working with in-app purchases, Apple requires that your App ID does not include a wild card, such as 76P4G6KX56.*. You are required to have a unique App ID, such as 76P4G6KX56.com.dragonforged.ufo. If you do not have a unique App ID, you need to create one. Use the following steps to create a new unique App ID:

1. Navigate to `https://appstoreconnect.apple.com/` in your web browser, and select your app from the list.

2. Select App Information from the column on the left.

3. Fill in the required information about your app.

4. Click Submit.

5. Click Configure next to the listing, and make sure In-App Purchase is turned on (it should be on by default).

Setting Up

We begin by requesting a list of products from our app. First, add the StoreKit framework to your project. We will be modifying our existing UFO project from the previous chapter; you can follow along in your own project if that is more convenient.

Important   In-App Purchase does not work on the simulator; all testing needs to be done on a device.

Create a new class called UFOStoreViewController. We will use this class to display a store to the user. Set up the source code file to match the following:

```
import UIKit
import StoreKit

class UFOStoreViewController: UIViewController {
    var productsRequest: SKProductsRequest?

    @IBOutlet var storeTable: UITableView!
}

extension UFOStoreViewController: SKProductsRequestDelegate {
}
```

As you can see, we imported the StoreKit header. Set up the SKProductsRequestDelegate, and create a new object to hold on to the product request. We need to create a way for the user to access the store, so go ahead and add a button to the main screen and relevant code to present the new view controller.

Retrieving the Product List

Modify the viewDidLoad function of our new store view controller to begin a new store request using the product identifiers that we set up in App Store Connect. You might need to modify your product identifiers to match the ones that you set up in the previous section.

```swift
override func viewDidLoad() {
    super.viewDidLoad()

    let productIdentifiers: Set<String> = [
        "com.dragonforged.ufo.newShip1",
        "com.dragonforged.ufo.subscription",
        "com.dragonforged.ufo.newShip2"
    ]
    let productsRequest = SKProductsRequest(productIdentifiers:
    productIdentifiers)
    productsRequest.delegate = self
    productsRequest.start()
    self.productsRequest = productsRequest
}
```

The product request is released in the delegate callback, shown next. Right now, this method just prints your product information to the console and logs any invalid products.

```swift
func productsRequest(_ request: SKProductsRequest, didReceive
response: SKProductsResponse) {
    for product in response.products {
        print("Product title:", product.localizedTitle)
        print("Product description:", product.
        localizedDescription)
```

```
        print("Product price:", product.price)
        print("Product id:", product.productIdentifier)
        print("\n\n")
    }

    for invalidProduct in response.invalidProductIdentifiers {
        print("Invalid product identifier: \(invalidProduct)")
    }

    productsRequest = nil
}
```

Note   Although you can retrieve a list of invalid product identifiers using the code in this section, there are no associated errors to determine why a product is being flagged as invalid. Under most occurrences, the product ID is mistyped, or not enough time has passed for the product to be distributed to the servers.

If you were to run the game now and navigate to the store, you should get output similar to the following:

```
Product title: Ship+
Product description: Paint your ship and show off to your
                     friends
Product price: 8.99
Product id: com.dragonforged.ufo.newShip1

Product title: Subscription
Product description: A subscription service
Product price: 1.99
Product id: com.dragonforged.ufo.subscription
```

Note   It can take several seconds to get a response from the product request. Best practices dictate that you should present your user with some sort of loading indicator.

These are all the steps required to retrieve your products from Apple's servers. In the next section, we present this data to the user using a standard table view.

Presenting Your Products to the User

We begin by adding a table view to our store view controller. Don't forget to hook up the data source and delegates, as required. We also add a new property to our class to hold on to the products. Create a new array property named productArray.

```
var productArray: [SKProduct]?
```

Set the product results to it and reload the table in the productsRequest method.

```
productArray = response.products
storeTable.reloadData()
```

Add the two required table view delegate and data source functions to your class, as shown in the following code snippets:

```
extension UFOStoreViewController: UITableViewDataSource {
    static var currencyFormatter: NumberFormatter = {
        let currencyFormatter = NumberFormatter()
        currencyFormatter.numberStyle = .currency
        return currencyFormatter
    }()
```

```swift
func tableView(_ tableView: UITableView,
numberOfRowsInSection section: Int) -> Int {
    return productArray?.count ?? 0
}

func tableView(_ tableView: UITableView, cellForRowAt
indexPath: IndexPath) -> UITableViewCell {
    var cell: UITableViewCell

    if let dequeuedCell = tableView.dequeueReusableCell(
    withIdentifier: "Cell") {
        cell = dequeuedCell
    } else {
        let subtitleCell = UITableViewCell(style:
        .subtitle, reuseIdentifier: "Cell")
        subtitleCell.selectionStyle = .none
        cell = subtitleCell
    }

    let cellText: String
    let cellDetailText: String

    if let product = productArray?[indexPath.row] {
        Self.currencyFormatter.locale = product.priceLocale
        let priceText = Self.currencyFormatter.string(from:
        product.price)
        let titleComponents = [product.localizedTitle,
        priceText]
        cellText = titleComponents.compactMap{ $0
        }.joined(separator: " - ")
        cellDetailText = product.localizedDescription
    } else {
```

```
            cellText = "Unknown Product"
            cellDetailText = ""
        }

        cell.textLabel?.text = cellText
        cell.detailTextLabel?.text = cellDetailText

        return cell
    }
}
```

The var at the top configures the currency formatter that will be used by cells to format product prices. The first function simply returns the number of products that we retrieved from Apple's servers for the number of rows in the table. When we display them as a cell, we use the built-in .subtitle style. We set the main label to the product title and price and use the detail label to display the description. All that is left is to add a reload table method to the end of the productsRequest method. Upon running the game again, you should have a table view that correctly list the two in app purchases that were previously set up in App Store Connect.

Note   Although the API returns a localized title and description, it doesn't localize the price. You need to take this extra step yourself in international apps.

Purchasing a Product

In the previous section, we learned how to add products to your app. Without the ability to purchase these products, our implementation is only partially complete. In this section, we look at how to handle purchasing products directly through your app.

Purchasing Code

The first thing that we need to do is make our store's view controller class conform to the SKPaymentTransactionObserver protocol. After that is done, we modify our existing viewDidLoad method. We add ourselves as a new transaction observer. Additionally, we perform a test to make sure that we can make payments on this device and, if not, display a UIAlert to inform the user.

```swift
override func viewDidLoad() {
    super.viewDidLoad()

    SKPaymentQueue.default().add(self)

    guard SKPaymentQueue.canMakePayments() else {
        let alert = UIAlertController.init(title: "", message:
        "Unable to make purchases with this device.",
        preferredStyle: .alert)
        self.present(alert, animated: true, completion: nil)
        return
    }

    let productIdentifiers: Set<String> = [
        "com.dragonforged.ufo.newShip1",
        "com.dragonforged.ufo.subscription",
        "com.dragonforged.ufo.newShip2"
    ]
    let productsRequest = SKProductsRequest(productIdentifiers:
    productIdentifiers)
    productsRequest.delegate = self
    productsRequest.start()
    self.productsRequest = productsRequest
}
```

Next, we need to add a didSelectRowAtIndexPath function to register selection events in our table view.

```
extension UFOStoreViewController: UITableViewDelegate {
    func tableView(_ tableView: UITableView, didSelectRowAt
    indexPath: IndexPath) {
        guard let product = productArray?[indexPath.row] else {
            return
        }

        let payment = SKPayment(product: product)
        SKPaymentQueue.default().add(payment)
    }
}
```

If you were to run the app now and select a table row, you would get a confirmation alert. However, we have not yet written any code to process this transaction, nor have you set up a test user, so this is as far as you can currently get.

Purchasing Multiple Items

Apple has made it easy to allow your users to purchase multiple items at a time. The following code snippet can be used to bulk purchase multiple quantities of an item at one time, such as a user purchasing five packs of 100 gold.

```
if let product = productArray?.first(where: {
$0.productIdentifier == "com.dragonforged.rpg.100gold" }) {
    let payment = SKMutablePayment(product: product)
    payment.quantity = 5
    SKPaymentQueue.default().add(payment)
}
```

Processing a Transaction

After your user has requested a purchase, there are several steps that you need to take in order to ensure that their purchase is completed successfully. First, we implement the required method from the SKPaymentTransactionObserver. As you can see in the following code example, we test the current transaction state and then call some new functions, depending on whether the transaction succeeded, failed, or restored:

```swift
extension UFOStoreViewController: SKPaymentTransactionObserver {
    func paymentQueue(_ queue: SKPaymentQueue,
    updatedTransactions transactions: [SKPaymentTransaction]) {
        for transaction in transactions {
            switch transaction.transactionState {
            case .purchasing:
                print("Purchasing:", transaction)
            case .purchased:
                transactionDidComplete(transaction)
            case .failed:
                transactionDidFail(transaction)
            case .restored:
                transactionDidRestore(transaction)
            case .deferred:
                print("Deferred:", transaction)
            @unknown default:
                print("Unhandled case:", transaction)
            }
        }
    }
}
```

We need to implement some convenience functions to help streamline the process. If a transaction completed successfully or is restored, we need to record the transaction event, unlock the content that the user purchased, and perform some cleanup. If the transaction failed or was cancelled, we just need to perform the cleanup and probably notify the user that something went wrong.

```
func transactionDidComplete(_ transaction:
SKPaymentTransaction) {
    unlockContent(transaction.payment.productIdentifier)
    finish(transaction, withSuccess: true)
}

func transactionDidRestore(_ transaction: SKPaymentTransaction) {
    unlockContent(transaction.original?.payment.
    productIdentifier)
    finish(transaction, withSuccess: true)
}

func transactionDidFail(_ transaction: SKPaymentTransaction) {
    if let error = transaction.error as? SKError, error.code ==
    SKError.Code.paymentCancelled {
        SKPaymentQueue.default().finishTransaction(transaction)
    } else {
        finish(transaction, withSuccess: false)
    }
}
```

Next, we take a look at the unlockContent function. This is where things could differ in your actual app. In this example, we set a flag in the NSUserDefaults that we can check against to see whether the user has purchased a feature. Depending on how your app is structured, you might want to take a different approach, but no matter what approach you take, remember that you need to preserve the unlocked content through app restarts. See the section "Tying Everything Together in UFOs" for a sample on how to implement this approach.

```swift
func unlockContent(_ productId: String?) {
    switch productId {
    case "com.dragonforged.ufo.newShip1":
        UserDefaults.standard.set(true, forKey:
        "shipPlusAvailable")
    case "com.dragonforged.ufo.subscription":
        UserDefaults.standard.set(true, forKey:
        "subscriptionAvailable")
    case .some(let unknown):
        print("Unrecognized productId:", unknown)
    case .none:
        break
    }
}
```

The last step that we take for both successful and unsuccessful purchases is to perform a bit of cleanup on our transaction. The most important step in the following method is to call the finishTransaction method. We also log the results of the transaction for debugging purposes. Until you have called finishTransaction, the transaction remains open and in the system.

```swift
func finish(_ transaction: SKPaymentTransaction, withSuccess
success: Bool) {
    SKPaymentQueue.default().finishTransaction(transaction)
    if success {
        print("Transaction was successful:", transaction)
    } else {
        print("Transaction was unsuccessful:", transaction)
    }
}
```

Restoring Previously Completed Transactions

Often, your users will need to restore purchases that they have previously made. This could happen if they have reinstalled your app or have begun using it on a different device. It is important to always add a path for your user to download all of their content and unlock any purchases that they have previously made. Luckily, Apple has planned ahead for this scenario and has provided a simple method for restoring the user's purchases.

```
SKPaymentQueue.default().restoreCompletedTransactions()
```

This will repurchase all of your content as if the user had selected it from your store. You will receive appropriate callbacks to the paymentQ ueue(_:updatedTransactions:) method and can use your existing code to unlock content.

Test Accounts and Testing Purchases

If you were to try and purchase one of your items in the sandbox now, you would receive an account error. You need to first create a new test account in order to be able to test purchases without being charged for them.

To set up a new test user, you need to log in to App Store Connect (http://appstoreconnect.apple.com). Select the Manage User section from the main screen of App Store Connect; from here, select the option for a new Test User.

Test users do not need to use a real e-mail address, and you will want to select something quick to type and easy to remember, such as abc@def. com. Although you do need to enter a date of birth and other identifying information, there is no reason you cannot fabricate this data. Make sure to select the App Store as the one to test your localization against. You can make a new account for each region that you will test with.

Signing In with a Test Account

You cannot simply sign in with your test account in the Settings App. Doing so would result in you being forced to agree to the standard user agreement and being prompted to enter a credit card number. In order to resolve this issue, you need to use the Settings App to log out of your existing App Store account. After you are logged out of an account, you will be prompted to log in or create a new account during a purchase attempt. This is where you will enter your test account credentials.

Note   If you are testing on your primary device, don't forget to revisit the Settings App to log out of your test account before making real purchases or downloading updates.

Submitting a Purchase GUI Screenshot

We talked briefly about this step in the earlier sections of this chapter. Apple requires that you submit a screenshot of your in-app purchase before it will clear it for sale. There is some confusion about what Apple is specifically looking for in this screenshot. Apple is looking, in the simplest terms, for a screen capture proving that your in-app purchase is working as intended. For unlockable content, this would be a screenshot of the item being used, such as the user playing a purchased level or using a purchased item. However, sometimes your product might not be visible while being used. In cases such as these, Apple has accepted a screenshot of the store showing that the item has been purchased.

Note   You will not be required to submit a screenshot until you have finished writing and debugging your app and are ready to submit it for review.

Developer Approval

The last step that you need to take before your in-app purchase is ready to go is developer approval. Return to App Store Connect in your web browser, and navigate to the Manage In-App Purchase section of your app review page. There will be a new green button in the upper right-hand corner of the screen.

You will be prompted on how to submit your product. The following two options are available:

- Submit with Binary: This option will turn on in-app purchase with your next binary upload.

- Submit Now: This will allow you to submit a new product to an existing app.

Tying Everything Together in UFOs

Depending on the complexity of your in-app purchase, it could be very easy or very difficult to integrate it into your code. In UFOs, we have a very simple product, in which paying a one-time fee unlocks a different colored ship. When the user purchases the product, we store a key in our user defaults to reflect that. To unlock this purchase in code, we simply check for that key and then perform the required steps. To do this, we need to add some new art assets to the project. These have already been included in the Chapter 10 sample code (available at the Apress website).

After this is done, we need to modify our viewDidLoad function to change the ship's image. The following code snippet shows those changes:

```
override func viewDidLoad() {
    purchasedUpgrade = UserDefaults.standard.bool(forKey:
    "shipPlusAvailable")

    let playerFrame = CGRect(x: 100, y: 70, width: 80, height: 34)
    myPlayerImageView = UIImageView(frame: playerFrame)
    myPlayerImageView?.animationDuration = 0.75
    myPlayerImageView?.animationRepeatCount = 99999
    var imageArray: [UIImage]

    if purchasedUpgrade {
        imageArray = [UIImage(named: "Ship1.png"),
        UIImage(named: "Ship2.png")].compactMap { $0 }
    } else {
        imageArray = [UIImage(named: "Saucer1.png"),
        UIImage(named: "Saucer2.png")].compactMap { $0 }
    }

    myPlayerImageView?.animationImages = imageArray
    myPlayerImageView?.startAnimating()
    if let myPlayerImageView = myPlayerImageView {
        view.addSubview(myPlayerImageView)
    }
}
```

Summary

In this chapter, we covered StoreKit and in-app purchases. By leveraging StoreKit, you gain a number of ways to monetize your app, from expandable content to special upgrades for your users.

You should now feel confident adding a variety of products to your own in-app store. Although StoreKit isn't directly a part of Game Center or GameKit, you will undoubtedly find an in-app store an invaluable addition to your iOS, Mac, or Apple TV software.

We spent some time talking about ngmoco:) and its experiments and successes with the Freemium model. You should now feel confident with App Store Connect and all the actions that are required to fully set up an in-app purchase product, as well as the required code to get that purchase to display.

We looked at how to handle failures with purchasing and also the path of a success. We also explored some of the advanced topics, such as multiple purchases at once. Lastly, we saw how we integrated the entire experience into our UFOs demo app.

CHAPTER 11

Game Controllers

To say the least, Apple has had a long and complicated history with gaming on its platforms. When the iPhone first began to gain traction and the world was handed the first native SDK, gaming was clearly not a priority. Since that time and demonstrated by the technologies this very book is written about, Apple has come a long way. iOS Game Controllers were first announced at WWDC 2013 as part of iOS 7. Focusing on the screen while not being able to feel where gaming controls were proved difficult. Beginning with iOS 15, Apple would introduce new SDKs to handle on-screen Game Controllers.

Types of Physical Game Controllers

There are two general types of Physical Game Controllers, micro and extended. These may also be made available in wired (dock connector) or wireless (Bluetooth) models. Regardless of other physical and layout differences, all controllers will conform to the same types of input. It is important to note that extended controllers have more input controls than the standard controllers.

Micro controllers feature a directional D-pad, two primary buttons (A, X), and a menu button. Extended controllers feature a directional D-pad, four primary buttons (A, B, X, Y), three additional buttons (Menu, Options, Home), two sets of shoulder buttons, and two directional

© Kyle Richter and Beau G. Bolle 2022
K. Richter and B. G. Bolle, *Beginning iOS Game Center and GameKit*,
https://doi.org/10.1007/978-1-4842-7756-0_11

thumb sticks. Wireless controllers also feature a player indicator LED, which has four positions. Beginning with iOS 15, software controller functionality has been added to the platform, which is addressed later in this chapter.

Note   While a Game Controller can add a lot of functionality to your iOS, Mac, or Apple TV game, it is important to remember that they must be optional. In addition to any Game Controller support, the game must also contain all the required functionality through the touch screen, standard controls, or accelerometer where applicable.

When Game Controllers were first announced, very few companies were manufacturing them. By the time iOS 15 was being released, there were dozens of available options on the market from big names like Logitech and Razer to smaller companies and startups. Game Controllers with Apple compatibility now come in all shapes, sizes, and styles.

Connecting to Game Controllers

When a non-wireless controller (dock connector) is connected to a device, it is automatically detected. However, to detect a wireless controller, the app must specifically begin looking for one. The sample app adds a new button in the upper left-hand corner of the menu screen to toggle searching for a wireless controller.

A new IBAction is created for the "Find Wireless Controller" button. When the user first taps the button, the function startWirelessControllerDiscovery is invoked. The second toggle will end the search process with the class method stopWirelessControllerDiscovery.

```
@IBAction func findWirelessController() {
    findingWirelessController.toggle()

    if findingWirelessController {
        GCController.startWirelessControllerDiscovery {
            print("Wireless controller searching has finished")
        }
    } else {
        GCController.stopWirelessControllerDiscovery()
        print("Wireless controller stopped by user")
    }
}
```

When a new controller is detected, whether it is wireless or physically connected, a notification is fired, GCControllerDidConnectNotification. This notification and the partner notification for a Game Controller being disconnected should be registered at the first chance possible. In the sample project, this is done in the viewDidLoad: method of the UFOViewController class.

```
NotificationCenter.default.addObserver(self, selector:
#selector(setupControllers), name: Notification.Name.
GCControllerDidConnect , object: nil)
NotificationCenter.default.addObserver(self, selector:
#selector(setupControllers), name: Notification.Name.
GCControllerDidDisconnect , object: nil)
```

Note   When a controller is disconnected, it is recommended that the game automatically pause to allow the player to either correct the issue with the controller or return to touch-based gameplay. Do not forget to test disconnecting controllers during gameplay as part of the quality assurance process.

Upon receiving either of these notifications, a new function will be called setup Controllers:; this method allows the app to keep track of which controllers, as there may be more than one, are connected at any given time. The Game Controllers are available via the controllers function on the GCController object; this function will return an array of all the connected controllers. The value of the controller array is also saved to an array property for later use in the sample app.

```
@objc func setupControllers(_ notification: Notification) {
    gameControllerArray = GCController.controllers()

    if gameControllerArray.isEmpty {
        print("No game controllers found")
    } else {
        print("Game Controllers Found", gameControllerArray.
        count)
    }
}
```

Note   It is possible for the controllers to be detected before the notification is set up; it is therefore important to check the contents of the controller array when the notification is added to determine if there are any currently connected controllers.

Reading Data Through Polling

Once a controller has been connected to a device, the input from that controller needs to be read. In the sample app, UFOs, accelerometer data is read every 0.05 seconds. Since not all users will have access to Game Controllers, this behavior will still be needed even after adding Game Controller support. This makes the accelerometer polling method ideal for reading data from the Game Controller. Modify the existing motionOccurred: function in UFOs to add Game Controller functionality.

First, the game must determine if the player is using a Game Controller; this is done through determining if the device is currently connected to any Game Controllers; in real-world applications, you may want to provide the user with an option. In the event that one or more Game Controllers are connected, the last one in the array is used. In your own apps, it may also be beneficial to allow the user to select which controller they intend to use. A new controller object is created, and the last controller in the array is stored into it.

The UFOs game has two primary functions: the first begins the tractor beam action, and the second moves the ship from location to location on the screen. For the purposes of the demo, the Y button on the controller will be used to engage the tractor beam. Since the tractor beam remains on as long as the button is continually pressed, a bool is created to keep track of when the button is currently pressed/depressed.

The action from the button is simply passed to the touchesBegan function, which is the same function that controlled the tractor beam when handling touch events. The benefit to this type of approach is that the touch events will still work even with a controller connected. Since both standard and extended Game Controllers have a Y button, there is no specific code required to handle the different controllers.

When using a standard controller, the D-pad will be used for movement. However, the thumb directional pads on the extended Game Controller make for a better experience when controlling the ship so the app will use those when available. This is done through the property extendedGamePad; if this value is non-nil, then an extended controller is currently connected.

Like the A, B, X, and Y buttons, the D-pad values can be accessed via a property on the GCController object. However, the D-pad returns a float value of 0.0 to 1.0 for X and Y axes. This value can be used in place of the accelerometer value used when a Game Controller is not hooked

up. Hooking up the values for the thumb stick for the extended Game
Controller are nearly identical but are stored under the extendedGamepad
instead of the root gamepad property.

```swift
func motionOccurred(_ accelerometerData: CMAccelerometerData) {
    if let controller = /*parentViewController.*/
    gameControllerArray.last {

        //Testing for button press
        let pressed = controller.microGamepad?.buttonX.
        isPressed
        if pressed == true && gameControllerXHit == false {
            gameControllerXHit = true
            xButtonAction()
        } else if pressed == false && gameControllerXHit ==
        true {
            gameControllerXHit = false
            xButtonAction()
        }

        if let extendedGamepad = controller.extendedGamepad {
            accel[0] = extendedGamepad.leftThumbstick.xAxis.
            value * accelerometerDamp + accel[0] * (1.0 -
            accelerometerDamp)
            accel[1] = extendedGamepad.leftThumbstick.yAxis.
            value * accelerometerDamp + accel[1] * (1.0 -
            accelerometerDamp)
        } else if let microGamePad = controller.microGamepad {
            accel[0] = microGamePad.leftThumbstick.xAxis.
            value * accelerometerDamp + accel[0] * (1.0 -
            accelerometerDamp)
```

```
        accel[1] = microGamePad.leftThumbstick.yAxis.
        value * accelerometerDamp + accel[1] * (1.0 -
        accelerometerDamp)
    }
} else {
    accel[0] = accelerometerData.acceleration.x
    * accelerometerDamp + accel[0] * (1.0 -
    accelerometerDamp)
    accel[1] = accelerometerData.acceleration.y
    * accelerometerDamp + accel[1] * (1.0 -
    accelerometerDamp)
    accel[2] = accelerometerData.acceleration.z
    * accelerometerDamp + accel[2] * (1.0 -
    accelerometerDamp)
}
}
```

Note   The 0.0 value is determined when the D-pad or thumb sticks are at rest; previous to the Game Controller framework, developers found it necessary to design a "dead zone" around the at rest positions; with the Game Controllers, this is no longer necessary, and any value above 0.0 should be considered intended movement.

Data Callbacks

There are many circumstances where it doesn't make sense to poll for Game Controller input each time the game loop cycles. Luckily Apple has provided functionality for callbacks that can be set upon a value change on any physical button on a Game Controller. In the following snippet, a handler is set for the right shoulder button. When the button value is changed, this function will call the rightShoulderButtonAction:

```
controller.extendedGamepad?.rightShoulder.valueChangedHandler =
{ [weak self] button, value, pressed in
    if pressed {
        self?.rightShoulderButtonAction()
    }
}
```

In addition to setting up a callback per action, the callback can be shared across multiple buttons at once. This can be accomplished by creating a new block and setting it up as seen in the following code snippet. This will cause any action on the A, B, X, and Y buttons to result in the log statement being printed:

```
let buttonHandler:  GCControllerButtonValueChangedHandler = {
button, value, pressed in
    print("Handle action for \(button) pressed: \(pressed),
    with value: \(value)")
}
```

```
controller.extendedGamepad?.buttonA.pressedChangedHandler =
buttonHandler
controller.extendedGamepad?.buttonB.pressedChangedHandler =
buttonHandler
controller.extendedGamepad?.buttonX.pressedChangedHandler =
buttonHandler
controller.extendedGamepad?.buttonY.pressedChangedHandler =
buttonHandler
```

It is also possible to set up data callbacks for dealing with changing axis values with the D-pad or thumb sticks. This can be accomplished with the following code snippet:

```
controller.extendedGamepad?.rightThumbstick.valueChangedHandler
= { stick, xValue, yValue in
    print("Right Thumb Stick value did change: \(xValue),
    \(yValue)")
}
```

Pausing

If your game supports Game Controllers, it must also support the pause button that is found on all Game Controllers. Even if your game did not previously support pause, it becomes a requirement of having a Game Controller connected. Working with the pause button on a Game Controller is very simple and only requires a couple of extra lines of code.

```
controller.extendedGamepad?.buttonMenu.pressedChangedHandler =
{ [weak self] button, value, pressed in
    self?.togglePauseState()
}
```

Player Indicator Lights

Wireless Game Controllers also feature player indicator lights, as the Game Controller framework supports multiple controllers behind hooked up to a single device. Your game can support multiplayer functionality using a single device through additional wireless controllers. Each wireless controller will feature four LED lights which will indicate the player number. These lights are also used to let the user know they have successfully connected a wireless controller, even in single player mode.

To illuminate the first light of the wireless controller, letting the player know they are successfully connected, the following code can be used:

```
if controller.playerIndex == .indexUnset {
    controller.playerIndex = .index1
}
```

The playerIndex property can also be used to illuminate other player index values, from 0 to 3. Only one player indicator light can be toggled on at a time per controller.

Snapshotting

It may become necessary to create a snapshot of the controller input state. This can be useful not only for debugging but also for creating playback profiles or sending the controller data over a network. Snapshots are stored through an NSData representation.

```
let snapshot = controller.capture()
```

You can check if a controller is a snapshot using the isSnapshot property, seen in the following brief code snippet:

```
snapshot.isSnapshot // returns true
```

Virtual Controllers

Virtual controllers were introduced to the iOS platform as part of the iOS 15 updates. Virtual Controllers provide functionality and standardization of on-screen touch controllers. While virtual controllers are not new technology, prior to the release of iOS 15, users were responsible for rolling their own solution or deploying a third-party solution.

Figure 11-1. *From the WWDC announcement of virtual controllers*

In order to display a new virtual controller, a new instance of
GCVirtualController needs to be created.

```
let configuration = GCVirtualController.Configuration()
configuration.elements = [GCInputDirectionPad, GCInputButtonA,
GCInputButtonB]
```

```
let virtual = GCVirtualController(configuration: configuration)
```

Once created, it is possible to customize the image shown on a button.

```
let customButtonPath1 = UIBezierPath(rect: .zero)
```

```
virtual.updateConfiguration(forElement: GCInputButtonA) {
configuration in
    configuration.path = customButtonPath1
    return configuration
}
```

There may be instances where it makes sense to hide the controller button temporarily, such as when accessing a menu or while paused. This can be done with a quick call to the isHidden property as seen in the following snippet:

```
virtual.updateConfiguration(forElement: GCInputButtonB) {
configuration in
    configuration.isHidden = true
    return configuration
}
```

In order to connect the controller and display it on screen, a simple call to connect on the controller is performed. Once it is connected, the new handlers for the input need to be set up.

```
virtual.connect { error in
    guard let extendedGamepad = virtual.controller?.
    extendedGamepad else {
        return
    }

    extendedGamepad.dpad.valueChangedHandler = { dpad, xValue,
    yValue in
        print("DPad value did change: \(xValue), \(yValue)")
    }
    extendedGamepad.buttonA.pressedChangedHandler =
    buttonHandler
    extendedGamepad.buttonA.pressedChangedHandler =
    buttonHandler
}
```

When it is time to disconnect the controller, the virtual controller object accepts a call of disconnect.

```
virtual.disconnect()
```

These are all the steps required to create, display, interact with, and clean up a virtual controller. Apple has once again gone to great lengths to make implementing and working with this technology as easy and straightforward as possible. If your game would benefit from access to on-screen controllers, there is little reason not to implement this functionality.

Summary

In this chapter you learned about the Game Controller functionality from both physical and virtual controllers, beginning with the requirements of the framework to connecting and reading data. This chapter also covered topics such as pausing, player indicator lights, and snapshotting data. Game Controllers can be deployed using the same principles discussed on iOS, Mac, and Apple TV projects. You should now have a strong comfort level with this technology and how it can be quickly and easily deployed into your projects to give your users a standardized and universal means of input beyond the standard controls that come with the device.

Index

A, B

abductCow function, 15

Accelerometer motion, 9

Achievements, 79, 80

    add hooks, 100–102, 104–107

        custom GUI, 111, 113, 117–119

        failure, 119, 121, 122

        feedback, 108, 109

        notification, 111

        view and label, 109, 110

        Xcode, 112

    App Store Connect, 84

        configuration view, 86

        iTunes Connect, 85, 87–89

        modify, 92, 95, 96, 98

        presenting, 90–92

    benefits, 81

    Game Center, 82

    GUI *vs.* custom GUI, 82, 83

    reset, 99

Application Programming Interfaces (APIs), 2

App Store Connect

    add, 50

    Add IDs, 265

    adding products, 265

    combine, 54

    configure, 49

    create, 50

    description, 263

    developer approval, 279

    edit, 53, 54

    product list, 267, 268

    product to user, 269

    purchase

        code, 272, 273

        GUI screenshot, 278

        multiple items, 273

        restore, 277

        transaction, 274, 275

    score format, 51, 52

    set up, 259–261, 266

        auto-renewable subscriptions, 261, 262

        iTunes Connect, 264

        non-consumables, 261

        non-renewable subscriptions, 262

    test account, 278

    test users, 277

    UFO, 279

App Store Connect portal, 24, 25

    configuring, 26, 27

Asynchronous games, 217

Printed in the United States
by Baker & Taylor Publisher Services